Unbecoming Ourselves

Unbecoming Ourselves

Discovering Peace through Label Liberation

Heather Schenck

A Heart Awakened

December 2024

Edited by Amnet Author Services, Daniel Greening and Mirela Petalli

Cover design by Nicholas Schenck

ISBN: 979-8-3306-6601-0

For my partner, Alex.
Thank you for reminding me of my goodness. Your constant
support has changed my life for the better. I love you so much.

For my children Jack and Everly.
You have unknowingly contributed to my deepest awakening.
You are worthy of love and belonging exactly as you are. I love
you dearly.

Chapter 1: Who Are You?

Paradise is our primordial pure consciousness, which is free of all limitations but embodies the infinity of the divine.
—Anam Thubten

Am I a bad mother? Maybe my children are better off without me.

A familiar wave of panic starts to roll in over my body.

Another meal goes uneaten by my older child. Never mind that I am the only parent to these children at home right now, or that I am completely depleted of energy. Alex has been gone for only ten days so far, and I already feel like I'm losing grip on my sanity. Frustration builds inside me, as I ride the waves of panic, which is quickly followed by guilt.

What kind of mom gets mad when their child refuses to eat a meal? This can surely be added to the inventory of proof that I am, in fact, a bad mother.

Grabbing his plate with mounting agitation, I knock the uneaten food into the trash can and hurl the plate into the sink. The tension inside my body rises like a pressure cooker threatening to explode, and I clench my teeth in an attempt to keep these horrible thoughts and feelings hidden.

Ignore the body. Shut it down. It can't be trusted. The indelible mark that childhood and young adulthood left on my body are scars that can't be seen, only felt.

But my efforts to contain it all are ineffective, and my body reacts against my own will. The tears come pouring out, and my breath quickens, my whole body shaking as I gently slide myself safely to the floor. I come undone into a trembling, heaping mess of snot and tears. Cradling my head in my hands, I finally begin to sense some relief as the pent-up energy exits my body.

The wave of emotion begins to recede, and I wipe away the mess from my face. Jack appears bewildered by my embarrassing display of emotion, and Everly is shaking her rattle in her bouncy chair. Collecting myself once again, I push myself off the floor, resolving to turn this morning around with our new daily walk around the neighborhood. Smiling at my children, I reassure them Mommy is okay and ask if they are ready for our walk. I worry my mother-in-law has heard my meltdown from her home office in our basement.

Good moms would be able to handle this situation better than I am. I need my mother-in-law to see me as a good mom.

Keeping my mother-in-law and my children safe has become my main job ever since Alex, my husband, has temporarily moved out. This new Coronavirus has threatened the lives of everyone, and his mother's age puts her at high risk for serious complications. After many emotionally charged discussions, Alex and I decided it is best that he moves out until we feel safe, since he works as a nurse in the

COVID ICU. His mom lives with us, and we couldn't bear the thought of him potentially infecting her with the deadly virus. I feel responsible to keep everyone healthy and safe from this invisible, ruthless predator. The pressure suffocates me.

I need to be a good daughter-in-law, a good wife, and a good mother.

My kids, fastened securely in the stroller, and I head down the driveway and out of the cul-de-sac.

Ten days—it's only been ten days that Alex has been gone. I have no idea how long this will go on. I hate hearing his stories about what's happening at work; it's yet another burden I don't have the strength to bear. Another young man in his early forties had gone into cardiac arrest and passed away last night, despite Alex and his team's efforts to resuscitate him. It happened suddenly. Like many COVID patients, he died alone in a double occupied hospital room, without his family there to comfort him in the end. No visitors are allowed in the hospital, even when they're dying. Alex said one of the most difficult parts of the postmortem care for him was peeling off the pictures of the young man's children from his hospital bed and placing them inside the body bag with the patient. COVID has claimed yet another life in this ICU.

I wish I could only feel proud of Alex for courageously showing up in those ICU rooms to care for those patients, but I mostly feel angry and scared. I'm a terrible wife and a horrible mother.

I have always failed to meet my own expectations of myself. I've never quite met the self-imposed requirements of the identities I strive for. There is nothing more important to me right now than being a good mother, which has been increasingly difficult since the start of the pandemic.

We reach the end of the block, and I decide it's time to turn on a podcast I have recently discovered, called "Secular Buddhism."

It focuses on practical applications of various Buddhist concepts and has become an anchor for me through this stormy time. The three of us stroll around the neighborhood, listening to Noah Rasheta, lay Buddhist minister and host of the podcast, discuss groundlessness.

I learn that groundlessness illustrates the nature of impermanence, the constant change throughout our lives. Fearing uncertainty, we cling to things in a desperate attempt to halt our descent, but we continue to fall. The fear of uncertainty in my life right now is agonizing. I notice I'm clinging to being a "good mom." Constantly trying to check off boxes, I am deriving the majority of my self-worth from my ability to measure up to my perception of this "good mom" label.

A little arm reaches out from the stroller, my daughter's hand brushing the overgrown pine tree branches extending out onto the sidewalk. Recently reintroduced to the sun after the spring snow melted, the branches covered in prickly green needles react to her stroke by enthusiastically rebounding back up to the sun.

Noah compares groundlessness to a game of Tetris, in which we have no control over which piece we get next, so the best we can do is fit the shape we have just then. It is more skillful for us to embrace the uncertainty and release our grasping, since clinging does not serve us well. A skillful Tetris player obtains the highest score possible while eliminating rows of blocks. A skillful life player, from a Buddhist perspective, makes intentional choices that put them on the path to enlightenment or liberation from suffering.

The concept of groundlessness resonates deeply within me. My relentless striving to be a "good mom" has left me feeling like I'm falling, desperately grasping anything that feels stable around me. As if this pandemic is not difficult enough, I'm judging myself every step of the way. This paralyzing self-judgment and the exhausting chase for acceptance and worthiness are not new to me; I've known this striving since childhood. I have yet to look at myself through my own eyes for self-assessment. Instead, I carry the same self-judgment through from my childhood. Back then, this self-criticism enabled me to escape the threat of ostracization and degradation. My siblings were often deemed "bad" because they broke the rules and dared to question the insanity. I learned from them by staying in line.

Be what they need me to be, not who I want to be.

This inner criticism has followed me throughout my entire life. Whereas once it served to keep me safe in an unstable household, it is no longer serving me. On our walk back home, I realize I have always derived my self-worth from perceived success in obtaining and maintaining various labels.

About a year and a half ago, I had decided to leave my position as a nurse in the pediatric Cardiac Intensive Care Unit. What led to this decision was a well-executed, but failed resuscitation event of a three-month-old infant. Codes were fairly common in the CICU, but this time it felt different to me. As a mother myself to my own children now, I struggled to concentrate during the rest of my shift, as I couldn't help but imagine what it must be like to lose a child.

I had a lot of job prospects, as I had already been a nurse for six years to people of all ages. Finding a new job wasn't difficult; what was difficult was letting go of the Cardiac Intensive Care Unit nurse title. I loved being able to tell people I was a pediatric cardiac nurse. I took so much pride in that title, and letting go of it felt like mourning the death of a part of myself. Who was I without that label?

Whether it be the label of Critical Intensive Care Unit nurse or of a good mother, I have always clung to labels as if they are proof of my worthiness. Perhaps I am grasping for labels and identities out of fear of falling, giving myself the illusion that I have control over my life.

Arriving back at the house from our walk, I take the kids out of the stroller, and we go back inside for a snack. While chopping strawberries and arranging them on a plate for my children, I contemplate groundlessness and my grasping of labels. My constant striving to "become" is exhausting, which leaves me feeling frustrated and ashamed. Curiosity drives me to discover who I really am, why I cling to certain labels, and how to reduce the pain I experience as a result of that grasping.

****

"Who are you?"

When someone asks us who we are, we answer with labels; we name our occupation, our political affiliation, our sexual orientation and gender identity, our family role, our race and ethnicity and nationality, our hobbies and interests, our religious views.

We don't say these are the things we *do*, but rather who we *are*. We say, "I am a nurse," "I am a Democrat," and "I am an athlete." We live in a world where we over identify with labels, and it can damage our relationships with others and with our self-conception.

Many of us experience strained relationships with people we care about because of conflicting labels. We struggle to separate the humans in front of us from the decisions they make, because we see the decisions they make as who they fundamentally are. Many families and friends find themselves at odds with each other over their political beliefs, vaccine compliance, religious views, and more and experience a painful collapse of their relationships.

As individuals, we can cause our own anguish by clinging to the labels we and others have given to us. We believe that we *are* our labels, which leads us to constantly strive to live up to our idea of what that "should" look like. This causes us unnecessary emotional distress when we feel we aren't meeting our own expectations or when we need to let go of a label. I often fail to measure up to my idea of a "good mom," and that causes me a lot of anguish. When I have needed to let go of a label, such as when I left the CICU, it has caused me a lot of distress as well.

Fear of the unknown causes us discomfort, driving us to create stories to explain who we are and why things are the way they are. As parents, we lose our temper and yell, then tell ourselves we *are* a "bad parent." We fail to meet our expectations of ourselves at our jobs and tell ourselves we *are* "bad" at our jobs. As we fail to accurately observe events as they truly are, we shoulder all the blame and responsibility for our perceived failures. In an attempt to preserve the illusion that we are in control, we cling to our identities, even when those identities do not serve us well.

This self-inflicted discomfort is referred to as all-pervasive suffering in Buddhism. Siddhartha Gautama, most commonly referred to as the Buddha, identified three types of suffering. They include the suffering of suffering, the suffering of change, and the all-pervasive suffering. The suffering of suffering encompasses inescapable events such as physical pain, illness, old age, and death. The suffering of change includes our inability to hold on to what we desire forever, due to the nature of impermanence. All-pervasive suffering depicts our general dissatisfaction with our lives that stems from the ignorance of the way things really are.

Our perception of the events in our lives greatly determines the level of contentment and satisfaction we experience. Two people with similar circumstances can experience very different levels of satisfaction. Things exist as they actually are outside of our perception, then through our own personal lens. We never touch the true reality of events, as we always experience them through our unique perspective. We can't separate our lived experience from our direct perception of the events in our lives.

What would happen to our relationship with our labels if instead we said, "I practice nursing, I subscribe to Democratic views, and I run marathons?" Subtle differences in language help us distinguish between the temporary labels we create for ourselves and who we are at our core.

While attachments to labels cause us misery, they do simultaneously serve an important role in our communities and the world at large. When we are injured or ill, labels allow us to seek the help we need from doctors and nurses. When our vehicles break down, we need labels in order to search for a mechanic. If we need help in managing our finances, labels can help us seek help from a financial advisor. When searching for a partner, labels allow us to discover potential mates.

But labels do not serve us well in many situations. Our labels can cause us distress and hinder our growth and put strain on important relationships. We perceive our labels as a part of our core self, fixed and unchanging. The problem with this is that change is inevitable. Although some of our characteristics remain relatively stable over time, we are constantly subject to change based on our environment and our acquisition of new knowledge and experiences.

When we were children, adults asked us, "What do you want to be when you grow up?" The question was never what did we want to do, but rather, who did we want to become. The seed of needing to "become someone" was planted within us in our childhood, and we've spent our lives watering that seed by extricating our self-worth from this ideal.

As adults, we suffer in jobs that we no longer find joy in, because we don't know who we are without that title. We alienate ourselves from others who define themselves differently than we do. When we identify with our labels, we deny ourselves the opportunity for growth and self-compassion.

Consider for a moment someone who strongly identifies with being a lawyer. They are highly respected at their law firm and take on the most challenging cases. They say, "I *am* a lawyer" and derive a majority of their sense of self-worth from their ability to successfully win cases. When they come of age to retire, what toll could losing this label take on their mental health? Many people suffer from depression at this stage in life, partly due to their inability to reconcile who they are aside from their career choice.

What about someone whose career is causing them severe distress, but they struggle to change it because their career is entangled with their identity? Many people in high stress jobs such as nurses and doctors suffer extreme emotional distress but remain in their current positions because it feels like a threat to their sense of self if they lose that title. Who would they be if they no longer could say, "I am a nurse" or "I am a doctor"? Would they somehow be less themselves than before?

If we choose to make a career change that pushes us out of a role where we were the expert into one where we may be a novice, it is a daunting task itself. It is uncomfortable to leave our comfort zone and enter unknown territory. Beginning a new career requires a lot of learning and vulnerability, and this discomfort cannot be avoided. The part we do have control over, however, is how we see ourselves in relation to our jobs. If we say that our career is who we are, then when we choose to move on, we may feel like we are mourning the loss of a part of ourselves. When the self is entangled with our career choice, it can lead to emotional turmoil when we choose to make a change in our career.

The labels we give ourselves and others are just a facade, an illusion to what's truly underneath. Much like an onion, we have layers and layers that surround our core. Each layer is a label we give to ourselves and show to the world, but underneath all of our layers lies our true self, our true nature. Our true nature dwells in the space underneath all the layers we show the world. Whether it's a label we strive for or a label we're avoiding, we forget that they're just that: labels.

The goal is not to become shells of ourselves and abandon everything about ourselves that we value, but rather to change our relationship with the labels we give ourselves. How would our lives look if we were less attached to them? What limitations are we putting on ourselves by seeing ourselves as separate from others, permanent and unchanging?

Our identities are entangled with our own direct experience of our lives. Developing or strengthening mindfulness practices such as meditation and open awareness encourage the nurturing and discovery of the space between "I" and my experiences. Through these practices, we gain the unique perspective of observing our thoughts and emotions with less attachment and aversion. We can cultivate an awareness of our connection to all things and discover existence beyond the labels we see.

****

Exercises:

Each chapter will conclude with exercises, which will include guided meditations, journal entries, and other mindfulness practices. For the journal exercises, find a few quiet moments in your day and a cozy spot to reflect on the prompts.

Awareness Exercises:

1) Notice how labels play a role in your life and the lives of those around you.
2) Develop or strengthen your daily mindful meditation practice. Begin by finding a quiet space where you will be undisturbed, then establish a comfortable, seated position. Aim to meditate daily, as the benefits of mindfulness come from consistent practice. However, if you miss a day or even a few, be compassionate and kind to yourself and then begin your practice again. When you're first beginning a meditation practice, aim to meditate for at least ten minutes per session. However, any amount of meditation is better than no meditation.

Guided Mindfulness of the Breath Meditation:

Begin by finding a comfortable seated position. Settle into a posture that is upright and alert, yet comfortable—one that allows you to feel grounded and safe.

Allow your eyes to gently close or rest half open in a slight downward gaze and begin to rest in the present moment.

Do a quick scan of your body from head to toe, releasing any obvious tension. Relax the brow line, unclench the jaw, rest your shoulders down away from your ears, and relax the belly.

Take a couple of deep, cleansing breaths and then allow your breath to be natural. Notice how the body breathes itself naturally.

Bring your attention to wherever you most easily notice the breath. It might be the cool tingling sensation in the back of your throat on the inhale, the warmth on your upper lip on the exhale, or the rise and fall of your chest or belly.

If the breath is difficult for you to sense, you might consider placing a hand on your belly to stay with the breath. Let the breath be your anchor to the present moment.

Our minds so often dwell in the past or the future, they spend very little time paying attention to what is happening now. Our bodies are here, but our minds often aren't. So it's almost like we're living in a virtual reality. The breath is ever present, so our attention to it serves our awakening. It's always there, bringing us back to what's happening right here, right now so that we don't take for granted the sun on our cheeks or the sound of the birds chirping in the morning. Even though each moment of our lives is not pleasant, what's happening now is real. So we should bring our attention back to the breath, back to the realness of this very moment.

Rest your kind attention on the breath, and any time you notice your attention has wandered, sense gratitude for this moment of awakening and kindly return your attention back to the breath.

Each time your mind wanders, gently bring it back to your anchor, the breath, without judgment. Recognize that this busy mind is completely normal.

Be right here, in this moment.

You might explore bringing your attention to the beginning, the middle, and the end of each in-breath and out-breath.

Notice the space between breaths: when the in-breath has ended and the out-breath has yet to begin.

This breath, right here—hold yourself with compassion.

Noticing you've been swept away from the present moment is the practice.

Each time you return, dwell in the spaciousness of the present moment.

For the last couple of minutes, see if you can bring even more loving kindness and gratitude to yourself for taking time to be present today.

This very moment is all we have. This is where our opportunity for awakening and joy lives.

In this very moment.

Journal Exercises:

1) Who are you?
   a) Include both labels that you strive for and those that you try to avoid.
2) How have labels hurt you?
   a) Include labels that you avoid, as well as those you are/were proud of.
3) How have labels caused friction in your relationship with others?

Chapter 2: The Function of Labels

Kindness and curiosity, aspiration and acceptance—these are the keys to belonging.

—Sebene Selassie

"Freedom over fear" reads on many signs of protestors at the Colorado capitol building. Many people are getting impatient with the stay-at-home order enforced by our governor, claiming it is an infringement on their constitutional rights.

You're worried about your rights, but I'm worried my husband won't be returning home to his family.

Alex has been gone for three weeks now. His interaction with us is limited to FaceTime calls and the occasional overlapping of our shifts when he is coming on shift and my shift ends in the Neonatal Intensive Care Unit, where COVID hasn't made an appearance yet. During these rare and brief occasions, we greet each other with fear, longing, and six feet of space between us.

He's heard about the protests, and he's angry, rightfully so. Here we are suffering as our family is divided, all for the protection of other people. It's hard not to take other people's choices personally. It seems like every person who refuses to wear a mask, claims that COVID isn't real, or attends one of these protests is holding a metaphorical middle finger up to me and my family. Yet Alex keeps showing up in these hospital rooms, donning his used, one-time-use mask to hopefully save one more person infected with COVID. We can't help but agonize over how many of these protestors will end up as one of his patients, now that they've been in a crowded setting.

Many of the protestors wear the now iconic red "Make America Great Again" hat, showing their support for President Donald Trump. This worldwide pandemic has turned into a political issue, because of which we have found ourselves divided instead of united, some concerned about our freedom and the economy and the rest of us more concerned about safety.

Trumpers are going to destroy us. They are willing hosts to the virus, and their careless behavior is going to kill us all. They lack empathy for others and reason, even in the face of scientific evidence. That's not me, not my family. I believe in science. I care about the welfare of others.

Things at home are getting harder. My mental health has hit an all-time low, as the waves of depression and panic are coming more frequently and with more intensity: three weeks of going back and forth between work and home, hoping the deadly virus hasn't hitched a ride on the bottom of my shoes to come home and attack my children and mother-in-law; three weeks of maniacally sanitizing our groceries and everything else that comes inside our home; three weeks of managing toddler meltdowns and middle-of-the-night breastfeeding sessions without my partner; three weeks of trying to control what I can to stabilize myself in this quicksand; three weeks of harping on myself for being a bad mother; three weeks of the greatest fear I have ever experienced in my life, without my partner by my side.

I learn that my fear of uncertainty is the problem, not uncertainty itself, during our walk this morning. We stop by the neighborhood pool while the Secular Buddhism podcast plays on my iPhone, and Jack clambers up the picnic table to retrieve a book from the free little library just outside the pool entrance. He makes his selection, then happily climbs back into the stroller with his prize. Noah's voice accompanies the three of us as we stroll around the neighborhood, suggesting that we strengthen our ability to adapt to changes in our lives. Fear of the unknown does nothing to prevent unexpected things from happening to us, so we should focus our energy on learning to accept change and that a lot of things are out of our control.

A little gray lump lies in the middle of the sidewalk just ahead of us. As we approach, the mysterious mass reveals its identity. It rests belly up, a tiny black beak amid a display of black and gray plumage, its talons uncurled, no longer grasping the safety of a tree branch. Its corpse is somehow ironically both simultaneously grotesque and beautiful. I pause for a moment in its presence, then maneuver the stroller off the sidewalk and around the creature, continuing our walk back home.

The fear of uncertainty is the theme of my life right now. I am in constant fear of me or my family contracting COVID and dying. I am in constant fear that I am failing as a parent, that I am not good enough for my children, that I am a bad mom. I'd give anything for someone to tell me for certain what will happen to us and whether I'm a good mother to my children. But if they did, would I trust it? How do I find this voice inside myself?

Once we're home, I look down at our newly curated daily agenda and announce to the children that it's time for arts and crafts. Jack and I have been crafting letter-shaped animals, each day a new letter and a new animal. We research interesting facts about the animal, then tape the animal shape to the wall. Today is N: Narwhal.

A Narwhal's tusk is actually a large tooth. We both find this fact amusing. Letters A through N hang in a row on my living room wall, mocking me with a reminder of how many days have passed since our lives were flipped upside down.

Everly is on the floor next to us playing pot surprise, in which she discovers random household items that I have put inside a cooking pot, a game that I have facetiously named after cannabis. Alex and his colleagues call the drug screens they run on their patients the "Colorado positive" since a large percentage of the population here uses it now. Her bright eyes light up as she discovers the cake decorating tool she likes to use for teething.

As long as it's not my nipple.

I am exhausted. My eyes are still puffy from crying to Alex on the phone last night. I told him I couldn't do this anymore, that I needed him home. I told him I felt like I was losing control of myself, that I wanted to run away from it all. I feel mentally unstable and extremely vulnerable. Our physical separation in the middle of this chaos is taking its toll on me. I am broken, and I don't have the right tools to put myself back together. I've grown resentful of him for being gone, for continuing to care for COVID patients as it means he can't be with us. I feel like he is choosing his job over me and the children.

I am not worthy of love. I am not wanted.

As a child, I felt like I had to "perform" to be accepted and loved; my value was not inherent. It was derived from my ability to follow the rules and to share their beliefs—to not question things, to not think for myself. Now I'm a mother who needs to mother myself, but the familiar internal voice is full of judgment and shame.

The stress is showing in my care of the kids. My patience is gone, and I find myself yelling at them frequently. This is not what I want for my family. My children deserve a kind, patient, compassionate mother.

I am a bad mother. Good moms never yell at their kids. My kids deserve better than me.

I beg and plead to Alex to give me a definite timeline of his return to us. However, he says, based on what he's seeing in the ICU and what we're reading in the news, this pandemic could continue much longer. After a lot of deliberation, we decide he is going to come home in two more days. Two more days will be a long enough time period between his most recent shift to get over and for symptoms to show if he is infected with the virus. I'm done waiting and want him to come home now. He tells me it's *only* two more days, but to me, that feels like an eternity.

The clock on the oven reads 12:10; I'm ten minutes late for lunch according to our schedule. I clean up our craft scraps and make sandwiches. I invite my mother-in-law, who is currently on lunch break, to join us for a picnic in the backyard.

The sun kisses our skin, and the temperature outside is a bit chilly but comfortable with a light sweater. For just a moment, everything seems like it just might be okay, as I watch Jack eat around the crust on his sandwich and Everly gaze at a bird fly in the sky, while Francie and I talk about Alex's homecoming.

I can do this for two more days. I can be a good mother.

Our backyard picnic has concluded, and Everly is down for a nap; so for either twenty minutes or two hours, I am a mother to only one child. I constantly find myself in disbelief at how much energy Jack has. I don't know how older or single parents handle an energetic child. We're back inside, playing with his favorite toy cars and trucks. Jack has such a fondness for construction vehicles that I have learned more about trucks in the past year than I have in my entire life.

I love being a mom, but sometimes I worry that I'm not cut out for this responsibility. I constantly worry that I am going to damage them, to give them a reason to feel hurt by me. I don't want them to know the pain I know. The uncertainty of parenting destroys me inside.

I don't even realize I've checked out until I hear my son shout, "Mommy, wake up!" At his command, I return to the present moment and drop to the floor, Hot Wheels car in hand, ready for a race with my son.

Mommy's trying to wake up, darling; Mommy's trying.

****

Historically, labels served to protect us from potential predators. When our early human ancestors hunted and foraged for food, it was imperative that they recognized which animals were a threat to their safety and knew how to protect themselves. Early forms of language enabled them to communicate to their group about existing threats and how to avoid them. Their primordial instincts and use of language to educate the group were necessary for the continuation of the species. During these times, the use of words and labels was very skillful for survival purposes.

In modern times, we still face dangers and potential threats to our safety, but not to the same extent that our early ancestors did. Generally speaking, our lives are no longer in constant, immediate danger. Many of the same biological processes, however, still exist in our brains today, which prime us to be on alert for potential threats in our surroundings. This creates a world in which we label others as "like me" or "not like me"; however, this distinction no longer necessarily serves us in a way to protect us from danger. We identify with labels such as our political affiliation, race, and sexual orientation and describe others who use those same labels as "like me." We characterize people who identify with different labels as "not like me." This distinction creates the concept of an ingroup and an outgroup in society, or us versus them. Many of us gravitate toward people who we consider our ingroup based on their labels and avoid people who we consider to be the outgroup.

Discovering the exact location in the brain and origin of the sense of self is a topic that has long been studied by scientists. In a meta-analysis in 2006 by Northoff et al. (440–57), using PET and fMRI imaging between 2000 and 2004, it was suggested that the sense of our core self is mediated by the cortical midline structures (CMS). These structures are also responsible for our ability to regulate our mood and express emotions, recognize facial expressions in others, recall past experiences, make decisions, plan for the future, and other executive functions. Other areas of the brain such as the amygdala interact with the CMS and can change the way we perceive ourselves and others. The amygdala has been considered the fear center of our brain as its primary function is to detect and alert us of potential threats in our surroundings. A study conducted by Kim et al. (421–30) demonstrated that learned fear is maintained by the amygdala, even after the conditioned stimulus is removed (2013). Once our cortical neurons have developed a learned fear pathway, the fear-inducing stimulus no longer needs to be present for us to have a conditioned fear. In another study using fMRIs to examine the effect of psychosocial stress on the human brain, it was discovered that there was increased amygdala functional connectivity to the CMS during the stressful event and an hour later (Veer et al. 2011, 1534–41). These findings suggest that fear can play a role in our brain's development of our sense of self.

Fear was the driving force behind my own misconception of Trump supporters and categorizing a diverse group of individuals as "not like me." By separating them into an outgroup, I inadvertently made erroneous assumptions about everyone in that group. I made the assumption that every Trump supporter disregarded science and lacked compassion for others. These beliefs that I held were the breeding ground for deep-seated anger, which only made my own individual suffering worse. At the time, it felt important to me that I create a self that was completely separate from "them," but now I recognize one key element that connected us all: fear. Many people who were protesting against the lockdowns were also driven by fear, the same emotion I was experiencing. We can't stop fear from arising, as it is a biological survival mechanism we've evolved with. What we can do, however, is recognize when fear is present in our bodies. We can learn to recognize it in others, then have more beneficial communication instead of alienation.

The ability to communicate potential dangers to others in our species was essential to our survival in early human history. Homo sapiens have an incredible ability to perceive and convey complex messages to other humans. Two major centers in the human brain responsible for language comprehension and language production are Broca's area and Wernicke's area. Crucial to speech production, Broca's area contains mirror neurons, which are widely understood to fire both when an action is executed and when it is only observed. Mirror neurons have also recently been discovered to play a role in voluntary vocalizations. Primate brains contain a Broca's area as well, and since they still exhibit involuntary vocalizations once Broca's area is severed, it has been presumed that Broca's area is responsible for intentional vocalizations. The size and structure of Broca's area are different in humans, however, and the differences are believed to lead to higher levels of integration of information. Wernicke's area, while also present in apes, is also larger in structure in humans and is believed to assist in processing word meaning (Rilling 2014, 1–3). These advanced characteristics allow us to use spoken language to convey important messages to each other, such as who or what can potentially cause us harm.

There are several ways in which scientists have attempted to explain what makes human brains unique, such as using the encephalization quotient (EQ).The EQ is calculated by comparing brain and body weight to the expected brain weight. An EQ of 1 represents a mammal with an expected brain size for the body weight relative to their species, whereas an EQ of less than or more than 1 represents an animal with a smaller or larger brain than expected for the body weight in their species. Australopithecus afarensis, widely believed to be the earliest known predecessor to the human species, had an EQ between 2.5 and 7.5. Modern humans have the highest EQ of their ancestors of 7.4–7.8, and in some respect, EQ seems to be a reliable indicator of intelligence. There are, however, multiple examples of outliers that this theory does not support, such as why dogs and squirrels have similar EQs, even though dogs display higher levels of intelligence (DeFelipe 2011, 1–2). What is evident, however, is that human brains have evolved and grown rapidly over a relatively short time period. It's important to evaluate and consider the possible implications of this relatively rapid growth to gain insights into the root causes of human suffering.

Advanced cognition and language processing has been essential for Homo sapiens' survival as a species. By generating labels, or words, for dangers they witnessed, early Homo sapiens were able to avoid extinction and continued to evolve. In modern times, most of us live relatively safe lives. We live in homes with walls, ceilings, doors, and locks that protect us from inclement weather and from other people and animals that might harm us or take things we own. We have electricity and can see our surroundings clearly even when the sun has fallen and the sky is dark. We have a government and laws in place that protect our rights to our property and to our physical safety. We are undoubtedly in a much different situation than our early ancestors were. We still have mental processing, however, that although once crucial to our survival, now serves to give us a false sense of security in situations that may not even be an actual threat to us.

The dangers of using labels this way can clearly be seen throughout history, and also in modern times. In times of slavery, white people utilized the fabricated label of race to justify the control and exploitation of black people. This label became so widely adopted into people's identities that although slavery was abolished in 1865, racism is still alive today. In the political landscape, it is also very apparent how labels can cause polarization between groups and lead to degradation of interpersonal relationships. Donald Trump's term in office cultivated animosity between supporters and non-supporters, and many people struggled to maintain healthy relationships with other individuals who were on the opposing side. When we adopt labels and integrate them into our core sense of self, we struggle to see beyond the labels of others and mistake people's labels as a direct reflection of who they truly are.

What becomes clear when we dive into the history of labels we assign, they isolate us from who we truly are and causes us to isolate ourselves from others. For community building and peace, it has become critical to our well-being as a species to cultivate a culture of inclusion and oneness with all living beings.

Acknowledging the problem with labels is important for positive changes to happen, but recognition is not enough to eradicate the issue. Since we are biologically programmed to form a sense of self and are constantly exposed to environmental triggers that induce fear that generates changes in our sense of self and others, extinguishing this problem will potentially take a lifetime of intentional work.

****

Awareness Exercise:

1. Begin a guided body scan practice.

Once you have an established daily meditation practice, aim to do a body scan at least once or twice per week, alternating with your other daily meditation. A body scan practice can be an incredibly powerful tool to bring you back into full awareness of the present moment by bringing awareness to sensations in the body. As you are guided through parts of the body in a body scan, it is important to pay attention to sensations that may include but are not limited to pressure/contact with the surface beneath you and other objects (your clothes, hair, etc.), temperature, physical sensations such as tingling, vibrating, pulsating, throbbing, twisting, stabbing, tightness, heaviness, lightness, expansion. If you notice numbness or can't sense physical sensations in any area of the body, that's okay too. There's no reason to judge any sensations or lack of sensations, just notice what is there (or isn't). It's also important to bring awareness to sensations as they change— did that spot where you felt a slight throbbing at the beginning of the scan still feel that way or has the sensation passed? Any time the mind drifts away from physical sensations to thoughts, kindly bring awareness to this as a normal activity of the mind, then gently bring the attention back to the body. Once you've spent time scanning through each individual part of the body, it's important to zoom out and examine the constellation of sensations throughout the entire body. Body scans are most often practiced while lying down, but you can choose the position that is most comfortable to you—seated on a chair, a cushion, or a bench on the floor or lying down.

Guided Body Scan Meditation:

Find a comfortable position, allow your eyes to close, and commit to being still for this practice. Allow yourself to arrive in the present moment by filling your lungs with a couple of deep, cleansing breaths, then allow your breath to be natural.

Allow your awareness to quickly scan through your body, feeling the contact of your body with the surface that you're on.

Now begin scanning the body from head to toe, spending time at each part of the body to deepen your attention and awareness of sensation. Beginning with attention to your head, see if you can notice any sensations present in the back of your head. Perhaps you notice where it makes contact with the surface beneath you. Now bring awareness to the top of your head and then your ears. Maybe you sense a tingling sensation on your head, your hair touching your ears, or a cool temperature on your ears.
If you don't notice anything, that is okay.

Now move your attention to your face. Soften your eyes, relax the brow line, unclench the jaw, let your tongue fall from the roof of your mouth, and let your mouth rest in a gentle smile.

Feel the physical sensations, the aliveness inside your mouth, and then your lips, your cheeks, your eyes, and your forehead. Try to feel these parts of your body from the inside out.

Notice the aliveness as it spreads down into your chest. Let your heart open, allowing space for anything to arise and pass through you.

If you notice thoughts or emotions arising, kindly acknowledge their presence and then gently return your attention to the physical sensations.

Draw your attention to your shoulders, allowing them to relax down away from your ears, letting go of any tension that may be present. See if you can feel your shoulders from the inside out.

Continue to slowly scan like this throughout the entire body, noticing and releasing any tension that arises. Continue to move your awareness down through the upper arms, the lower arms, the tiny muscles in your hands, the fingers, and then back up the arms and across the chest to the belly, the pelvic region, the upper legs, the knees, the lower legs, the feet, the toes.

Now zoom out, gaining awareness of the whole body of sensation, the aliveness. Relax with an open and receptive presence, allowing sensations to arise and pass through. Notice the breath again and how the body gently and naturally moves with it.

Take a moment to extend gratitude to this body, then allow your eyes to open when you are ready.

2. Choose one or two daily activities (such as washing dishes, walking to the mailbox, brushing your teeth, folding the laundry) to bring your mindful awareness to. Bring your attention back to the body during these moments and observe any physical and mental sensations that arise.

Journal Exercises:

1. How do you feel about uncertainty?

2. How do worry and fear play a role in your life?

Chapter 3: Observation

To pay attention, this is our endless and proper work.
—Mary Oliver

I should be feeling better than this now that Alex is home. He feels kind of like an outsider disrupting our routine.

I had been so desperate for him to come home, assuming his return would fix everything—fix all my pain. Instead, we are clashing. We are two helms trying to steer the same ship. I'm used to steering this ship alone now, and I feel agitated by the disruption.

Seeing the look on Jack's face as his father first walked up to our house brought me to tears. "Daddy," he said, gently whimpering, his little nose pressed up against the living room window. There was no proof his image of Dad was not just a mirage until we were wrapped in his comforting arms.

After waking from her nap, Everly was surprised by Daddy's arms reaching for her in her crib. She grinned from ear to ear and her eyes sparkled.

Together again, finally.

The excitement and relief I feel as Alex returns home to us soon disappears. He is home, but he isn't really here. He is physically here, but he is disconnected. We are outside enjoying the warm sun and gentle, cool breeze. I build a monster truck track in the sandbox; then the kids and I zoom toy trucks over the sandy ramps and obstacles. Everly giggles in the sweetest little voice, and I look toward Alex to acknowledge the tenderness of the moment, but he is gone behind his eyes. They are open, but they are not seeing.

"Where are you?" I implore him.

He's replaying another traumatic COVID death at work. He's retracing his steps, asking himself if he did everything right in the resuscitation. He's worrying about the family, how they will reconcile with the loss of their father, their partner, their son. He's angry at the owner of the meatpacking plant in Greeley that continued normal operation, going against public health guidance, leading to overcrowding in local ICUs with multiple COVID patients.

I feel bad seeing how this is affecting him, but I also feel angry and resentful. I have so much pent-up anger, and I don't know where to direct it. Who or what am I angry at? The virus? The first person to contract the virus and then begin the spread? President Trump for not encouraging isolation as advised by the Chief Medical Advisor? The news stations for spreading misinformation? My husband for temporarily moving out, leaving me feeling abandoned, so he could care for them? I am consumed by anger and frustration, wishing things were different than they are.

I understand that working in the ICU is Alex's job, that there was an expectation he'd continue to show up at work in the midst of the pandemic. I resent that he chose being a COVID hero over being a husband and a father. He abandoned me, not just while he was physically gone, but even now while he's home. I see him, but he's not really here. In his mind, he's still in those hospital rooms. His empty stare and disengaged interactions with us leave much to my imagination. I create stories to fill in the gaps, and the stories exacerbate my pain.

He doesn't want me anymore. He is choosing to be a COVID nurse over being my husband. If he's going to disengage with me, I'll disengage with him too.

I bitterly move about the rest of my day, not making eye contact. I try to convince myself that I will feel less angry at him if I just pretend he's still gone, if I expect nothing from him. But it doesn't work. Every indiscretion I notice adds fuel to the flame. Every time the children try to interact with him and he gives a disengaged, half-listening response; every time I start a conversation with him only to notice he's disappeared mid-conversation, every time I want to share a tender moment with my partner and am met with an empty shell, I feel angry. I feel the tension rising inside me again, like I might soon explode.

Don't feel, don't feel, don't feel. Push it down, push it down, push it down.

Strong and uncomfortable emotions have never felt safe to me. I've seen enough adults lose control when they were angry. I've seen them throw things, hurt my siblings and each other. I've heard their piercing words of judgment, blame, and shame. I have learned to leave my body when being in it didn't feel safe. I have learned to push my uncomfortable emotions down, to numb out. But eventually those uncomfortable emotions bubble to the surface, and I find myself exploding now. I'm falling into a pattern I've spent my life trying to avoid.

Alex and I are preparing lunch for the family together, and I'm making sandwiches. I ask him if he can slice some fruit for the side, but I don't get a response. I spin around and see him standing there, staring at empty plates on the counter. I say his name, but he doesn't move; he doesn't even blink. His name leaves my lips in an irritated tone and in a much higher decibel. Snapping back to reality, he asks me to repeat what I said to him.

Once again, I come undone. This time, it is not into a heaping blubbery mess on the floor. This time I come undone with rage. I accuse him of abandoning us, of leaving when we needed him the most. I describe the pain and suffering we have endured during his absence. I accuse him of choosing being an ICU nurse over a father and husband. I tell him that while I'm glad he is finally home, I still feel like he is gone.

He asks me why I'm attacking him and urges me to focus on the fact that he is home now. He reminds me that this wasn't solely his choice, that we made the decision for him to move out together. I am enraged by his distorted version of the truth.

Traumatic childhood memories are being replayed as I once again feel like someone has deemed me unworthy of love and belonging. Sometimes I feel like I never left that parking lot, like I'm still that scared girl, abandoned by her dad after he chose a life without her.

Consumed by the anger that has taken over me, I knock the kitchen chair over, and it goes crashing to the floor. I shout that him moving out was never the decision I really wanted, and he knew that.

My mother-in-law hears the commotion from the basement and guides the children downstairs with her.

I shout to Alex that if it were up to me, he would have quit his job, chosen his family instead.

"It's not that easy," he declares to me.

Bullshit.

I beg him to explain to me why his job is more important than me, than us. I plead with him to honestly tell me whether or not he still wants me, whether or not he wants this family.

He promises me he does. He tells me that working in the COVID ICU does not mean that he does not want to be with me. He describes how hard it is for him to see so much suffering at work, then come home and be what he needs to be for us. He apologizes for being disengaged and reassures me that he loves us, that he wants to be a part of the family.

I deflate upon hearing his words. My husband is suffering, and instead of being supportive of him, I've been angry at him.

I am a terrible wife.

The rage recedes from my body; then shame and sadness pour in. I burst into tears. I feel his embrace as I succumb to this wave of emotion. I notice how uncomfortable I feel with this level of vulnerability. I feel weak and defenseless. I recognize I'm experiencing discomfort with groundlessness, as my suffering is emergent from the lack of control I have over my life.

I hold on to Alex until I feel like I can stand alone again. The storm has passed, and we've found our way back to each other again. We collect our children from the basement, apologizing to them for scaring them. We explain that Mommy and Daddy were both feeling angry and should have talked about how we were feeling, instead of yelling and throwing things.

Good moms never yell. I am a bad mom. Maybe it's true; maybe I am evil and ugly, just like my mother used to tell me I was.

Intrusive thoughts accompany me the rest of the day, telling me that I am a bad mother and a bad wife. I can't skillfully handle my emotions regarding the pandemic and Alex's physical and emotional absence. I judge myself for having these emotions. I feel frustrated by myself, and I tell myself I should be able to do better—to *be* better. Labeling myself as a bad mom and a bad wife leaves me feeling paralyzed and helpless.

I lean on my sangha for support, a diverse group of Secular Buddhism podcast listeners. We have weekly Zoom meetings where we exchange support and relate Buddhist concepts to our lives. Recently, we had discussed emotions and our ability to recognize and name them. I learned there are over 100 emotions, but most people don't recognize many of them. Noah challenged us to count how many emotions we can recognize over a couple of days and how often we experience them. I recognized only two positive emotions and two negative emotions: happiness, excitement, sadness, and anger. After happiness, anger is the emotion I have experienced the most frequently.

Anger dominates my negative emotions. Anger feels safe to me: if I shield myself with anger, I can't get hurt. Anger lets me feel I'm in control. I consider that I might be transforming other negative, unwanted emotions into anger. I wonder what hides behind my anger, what emotions lurk behind that mask.

Attempting to reduce my self-judgment after the fight, I set aside meditation time. The kids have had 45 minutes of screen time today, so I get 15 minutes of meditation time.

Good moms don't let their children have more than one hour of screen time per day.

I am new to meditation practice, and I notice my mind is always very busy. I struggle to find even a moment when my mind isn't racing. Noah says mindfulness is like a jar of muddy water. If we let it rest, after some time, the sediment will drop to the bottom of the jar, and we will have more clarity. This clarity allows insight into our mind. I sit and let the thoughts slowly settle to the bottom, but soon discover I'm mixed up with thoughts again. While trying to withhold self-judgment, I set the muddy jar down to rest again. Because I tend to judge myself, this process is very difficult and requires consistent practice.

I begin to scan my body, noticing what is present. Opening to sensations in my body feels like dangerous territory to me. I spent my whole life learning to shut down what my body was telling me, for self-preservation. My body was a tool to make other people feel good about themselves. But the numbing out is no longer serving me. My body hasn't forgotten the fight with Alex. My brow is furrowed, my jaw is tight, and my shoulders are tense. I immediately recognize this emotion as anger and attempt to mindfully stay with the sensations. I drop the stories I told myself, that Alex doesn't love me and that I am a bad mother and wife. With loving awareness, I notice the physical sensations, without clinging to or rejecting them. The stories try to creep back in, and I imagine myself gently setting them back down and returning to the physical sensations. After a few minutes of this practice, I notice all the tension has left my body. Anger is no longer present in my body. I noticed when anger was present in my body, and I noticed when it left.

For a few short moments, I discover more spaciousness in my meditation, more peacefulness in the present moment without disruption. Then I am suddenly hit with a heavy sensation in my chest. My breath is shallow and rapid, and a tear rolls down my cheek. I feel uncomfortable, out of control, and vulnerable. The cause of this shift in sensation is unclear at first, but then she reveals herself.

There she stands—all three and a half feet of her. Her clothes are tattered, her hair unkempt, her eyes reluctant to make eye contact. She has bad posture, hunched over under the weight of emotional wounds. She looks like a younger version of me, at maybe seven years old. She introduces herself as Fear, and I instantly know she is the one hiding behind my anger.

I feel so uncomfortable in her presence, but I stay with her until my body relaxes. As I look into her eyes, she looks less scary now. I feel a kinship to her, realizing she's accompanied me most of my life. I have carried fear with me into every part of my life. I carry a fear of not being loved, of being abandoned, of "failing" as a mother, of being deemed unworthy. I don't like fear; I don't know how to befriend my fear. It doesn't feel safe. But my anger is hurting people, including myself.

The bell rings, signaling the end of my meditation, and I come back into the room. Sitting mindfully with strong negative emotions is new and difficult for me. I tend to react when I experience anger and fear, and this meditation practice has given me the opportunity to mindfully notice instead of impulsively react.

The four of us are eating pizza at the dinner table. Today was too emotionally exhausting to cook, so it is a delivery dinner night. Jack scrapes all the cheese off his pizza crust and shoves it in his mouth. It amazes me how a child can make delicious food look so unappetizing. I meet Alex's gaze, and we share a humorously disgusted face.

"Would you consider looking for another job?" I ask, trying my best to sound nonchalant.

I know this probably isn't the best time to ask, but he had admitted how negatively his job has been affecting him, so I jump at the opportunity.

"I'll look and see if there's anything out there," he says pessimistically.

While his response is less than reassuring, I take it as a win. I've spent eight years watching my partner suffer from job-related emotional stress. After graduating from the same nursing program, we both started working at a Washington DC hospital. He worked in the burn and trauma unit, where he witnessed a lot of devastation and suffering. When driving into work together, we'd frequently see caution tape around housing areas near the hospital and then facetiously joke that he'd be taking care of that patient shortly;

oftentimes, we were unfortunately right. He provided care for gunshot, stabbing, and burn victims. His job was to care for those patients during his twelve-hour shift, but the work always followed him home. I've lost count of the times I've woken him from work-related nightmares.

I wonder if he realizes how much his career has affected his personal life. I see how tightly wound his identity is to being an ICU nurse. Reflecting on my own personal struggle with letting go of being a cardiac ICU nurse, I feel compassion for him. I remember the struggle.

I sit across from him at the dinner table and feel pulled by two opposing forces: compassion for the man I love and judgment of him for allowing his identity with his job to cause him so much pain and suffering.

Like the rising sun that exposes what is lurking in the shadows, I see my hypocrisy. I see how tightly wound my identity is to being a good mother. I see how much pain it is causing me and how that likely also affects my family. I see so clearly how striving to be a good mother is a never-ending race with no finish line. The weight of that exhaustion sinks in when I realize just how long I've been running.

I don't want to be in this race anymore. I need to find an exit.

Here we are, two people stuck to their identities. I want to liberate myself, and he doesn't even realize he's stuck.

Buddha, help us.

****

Where do we start to let go of our sense of self? Buddhist teachings and practices offer much here. We are thinking beings. We spend most of our day thinking about what happened before and what might happen later, about our desires and our aversions. Incessant, unexamined thinking leads us to strengthen flawed assumptions about ourselves and others. It leads us to believe each thought we have is true, without taking time to assess the legitimacy of each thought or belief.

The alternative to thinking is observing—observing sensations, emotions, thoughts, and the world around us. Meditation and mindfulness practices cultivate an aware and curious mind. We learn to welcome sensations as they arise, without judging, clinging, or rejecting.

Through mindful observation, we realize that our thoughts are simply the products of mental activity, and not ultimate truths that we should believe. The incessant intrusive negative thoughts I experienced led me to believe that I was a bad mother. By practicing mindful meditation, I was able to open a space between "I" and my thoughts and feelings and detach from the "bad mom" label.

Meditation and its benefits are well known today. We can now find many guided mindful meditations through facilitators, books, videos, and apps. It can, however, be a daunting and frustrating task when someone begins a meditation practice, if not approached in a skillful way.

Neuroplasticity describes how our brains' neural networks change over time. Many scientific studies have shown significant structural and neural differences in the brains of long-term meditators versus non-meditators. One study demonstrated increased cerebral blood flow in the prefrontal cortex, parietal cortex, thalamus, putamen, caudate, and midbrain of long-term meditators versus non-meditators (Newberg et al. 2010, 899–905). These areas of the brain are responsible for impulse control, ability to hold attention, relaying and integrating sensory input, consciousness and alertness, cognitive function, learning, and motor control. The structure of the brain also appears to be different in meditators. In a literature review conducted by Fox et al. (48–73) many studies showed an increase in the thickness of the cerebral cortex and concentration of gray matter in long-term meditators (2014). Whether meditation caused these changes in meditators is not yet certain, but the findings suggest we can change our brains. We know neurons are plastic, and we can strengthen our brains by exercising them. The evidence strongly suggests meditation is an exercise that strengthens parts of your brain.

Mindful meditation begins before we even sit down and close our eyes; it begins with our intention. If our intention is to be happy and forget about our problems, it will not go well. This is a common misconception of the goal and benefits of meditation. Meditation will not make our problems go away. We will still experience sadness, anger, disappointment, pain, loss, grief, and every other unwanted emotion. In fact, we will become more aware of unwanted emotions. Meditation does not magically prevent suffering, but it changes our relationship with suffering.

Everyone experiences discomfort and anguish in their lives; everyone experiences suffering. There is nothing we can do to prevent it. It may rain on a day we planned a hike; our vehicle may break down on the way to work; we could trip and fall and break a bone; we will likely experience the loss of a loved one at some point in our lives; we ourselves may become ill unexpectedly; we could lose everything we've worked so hard for. Many of us believe the delusion that if we try hard enough, we can prevent suffering. The truth, however, is that none of us are immune. Wishing or asserting that suffering won't happen to us won't prevent it from happening; instead, it magnifies our suffering when suffering does happen to us.

A friend of mine experienced a lot of childhood trauma and suffering. Unlike her siblings, still caught in the cycle of trauma, she strived for excellence in her education, career, and marriage. She made it her life's work to learn valuable skills, break the cycle of family trauma, and create a peaceful home life for her children. Whenever major problems and struggles arose in her life, she asked me, "Why is this happening to me? I didn't do anything to deserve this." The truth is, she didn't do anything to *deserve* this pain and suffering.

Pain and suffering happens to everyone, everywhere, by the nature of existence. By personalizing the traumatic events that occur and believing we only get what we deserve from the universe, we set ourselves up for unnecessary suffering. The truth resolves our confusion, as suffering is not personal. If we wish to heal ourselves, we must learn and accept that some suffering is inevitable. Acceptance, unlike resignation, requires us to acknowledge that suffering is a part of life. Accepting that suffering exists and will happen to all of us doesn't propagate more suffering; it just changes our relationship with suffering. When we learn to accept that suffering is inevitable, the extra sting we feel for things "happening to us" fades. We no longer feel offended when suffering happens to us, because it no longer feels personal.

Once we acknowledge that wishing the suffering didn't exist magnifies our suffering, we can put that resentful, angry energy into comforting and healing ourselves instead. This radical acceptance of the way things are is the necessary first step in our journey to healing. Accepting suffering as a part of life opens a space where we can observe our minds and begin to recognize and name our unwanted emotions.

During meditation and throughout our daily activities, it helps to notice and examine our thoughts and emotions. Rather than clinging to them, positive or negative, we learn to observe them as impermanent states of mind. They arise in our bodies and then melt away. Then when the next emotion, sensation, or thought arises, we observe it arising and going away. We can imagine distracting thoughts as small children crawling into our laps; we can imagine gently setting those thoughts to the side and telling them, "I see you, and I will be with you soon."

When we feel unwanted emotions arising, such as sadness or frustration or fear, our instinct is to push it away. They make us uncomfortable, and we're worried about what we might discover if we look at them closely. We aren't really pushing unwanted emotions *away*; we are pushing them down inside ourselves to bubble up later in a harmful way. Those suppressed emotions could re-emerge as we struggle to maintain professionalism at work, unleash our emotions on our kids, or disengage from a partner who we feel devalues us. By pushing away our emotions, we prevent deeper understanding and healing. Had I recognized the feelings of unworthiness that were coming up for me during our fight that day, I could have tended to those emotions and then skillfully communicated them to my partner so that healing could occur.

Imagine you are lying in the grass on a warm day. You are comfortable and calm, gazing at the clouds. You notice clouds of different sizes and shapes, some fluffy, others streaky. You notice them, but you do not judge them. You do not think to yourself, "That fluffy cloud makes me uncomfortable so I'm going to pretend it's not there." Instead, you just gently notice the clouds slowly drifting by without judgment, without wishing one cloud would stay, without wishing another would go away.

This is how we sit in mindfulness meditation, observing our sensations and emotions as if they are just passing clouds. "I notice some frustration arising, and I feel a tightening in my jaw." Or "I am noticing a feeling of joy arising and feel my heart opening." We notice when sensations and emotions arise. We scan our body to locate any manifestations of these in the body; then we notice when they pass.

Thoughts will also incessantly intrude into our intentional space of awareness. It takes practice to be able to notice emotions and thoughts without judgment and to practice re-focusing on sensations. When beginning a meditation practice, it is common to sit for ten minutes with the goal of observing sensations, then hear the bell signaling the end of the meditation, only to realize we've spent our entire time thinking. This is where guided meditation can be useful, where a facilitator occasionally reminds the meditator to bring their awareness back to the present moment. Once we recognize our minds have strayed and we come back to our subject, such as the breath or sensations in the body, we do so compassionately. It doesn't do us any good to beat ourselves up about becoming distracted. Regret and shame only add to our suffering. Our minds often run on default mode, where we are constantly thinking, so this is why it feels so unnatural for us to try to observe instead.

Painful emotions and thoughts will sometimes arise when we sit in meditation or practice mindfulness. The more we practice, the more we strengthen our ability to recognize emotions as they arise, including so-called "undesirable" emotions such as fear, sadness, and anger. When we notice these emotions arise, we may experience shame. Shame can make us feel small, insignificant, powerless, and unworthy of love and belonging. Shame can be paralyzing and all-consuming of our energy. Shame is a thief of self-compassion, robbing us of growth. When we experience shame, we ruminate on things we can't control—things we've already done or things that we are feeling and thinking. When we are stuck in a cycle of shame, we are unable to make changes, unable to grow. When my self-judgment was at its worst, I was stuck in an anger-react-shame cycle. Feeling angry without mindful awareness, I would react harmfully instead of responding compassionately, then feel shame. I was stuck in this vicious cycle, not realizing that shame was robbing me of personal growth. Shame tricks us into believing that we are incapable of change and that the negative stories we've told ourselves about who we are, are true.

Mindfulness meditation presents us the opportunity to see ourselves as an outside observer. We may not necessarily like everything we see. We may feel tempted to turn away, to bury our heads in the sand, to remain ignorant. Observing ourselves may evoke difficult emotions, but that is very different from *believing* our thoughts and emotions. It takes great bravery to honestly look at our patterns of thoughts and behaviors, and it takes great skill and practice to skillfully handle the next step. When we notice shame arising, we can acknowledge its arrival and gently let it know that while we are aware of our imperfections we refuse to let it cripple us.

Observation gives us agency over our thoughts and emotions. We are the observer, and the thoughts and emotions are things we observe. We can create our own healing and growth by responding skillfully to what we observe. We can allow our thoughts and emotions to overwhelm us with crippling shame, or we can create tools with them. Our toolbox can contain special tools to recognize and skillfully handle our triggers, desires, and aversions. We can use these tools in every situation in our lives and act more skillfully, more in line with our core values.

We should observe our thoughts and emotions without attachment. Instead of telling ourselves, "I am angry," we should say, "I feel angry." If an intrusive thought arises, such as, "I am worthless," we should reframe that to "I am feeling unworthy." This subtle shift in language allows us to stop identifying with our thoughts and emotions. We should aim to be like an objective scientist, collecting data from an experiment. We can take note of thoughts, emotions, and sensations without allowing ourselves to identify with them. It requires practice to observe in a non-attached manner, and the ability to execute this distinction is imperative.

Noticing and observing is the practice we must come back to time and time again to see things as they actually are, and not let the stories we tell ourselves govern our happiness. The story I told myself when my partner was disengaged—that he did not value me and I was unworthy of love—was unfounded and made my suffering worse. Meditation is one piece of the larger system of mindfulness. Formal sitting meditation is an essential practice to cultivating mindfulness, and it is equally important for us to also bring this heightened level of awareness into our daily lives as well.

Similar to mindful meditation, other mindfulness activities should evoke a sense of acute, sharp awareness and attention to the present moment. Mindfulness can be practiced anytime, anywhere. While we are brushing our teeth, instead of letting our thoughts spiral, we can observe sensations. What do the toothbrush bristles feel like on my gums? What does the toothpaste smell like? Which section of my mouth am I brushing now? What is the quality of the amount of pressure I am putting on my teeth? While we are washing dishes, we can again practice mindfulness. What does the water feel like running over my skin? What does the water sound like coming from the faucet? What is the nature of the sound that comes from scrubbing a pan? What does the soap smell like? During meal times, we can also practice mindfulness. What does this bite of food taste like? Does it taste different on different points of my tongue? Is it cool or warm? Can I hear myself chewing, and if so, what does it sound like? What does it smell like? Do I feel satisfied yet, or am I still hungry?

We can ask ourselves throughout our day the simple question, "What is happening now?" This includes what we're adding to and what we're missing from the current moment. Are we adding unnecessary suffering to the present moment by believing stories we've created? Can we create such an acute awareness of each moment that we can even draw our attention to the lack of suffering, such as the lack of a toothache? We notice when we *are* experiencing physical pain, but can we draw our attention to the moments when we are free from pain? During the turbulent times in the beginning of the pandemic, my husband struggled to be present with what was happening now, yet many of those moments were opportunities for healing and joy. We can enrich every single, seemingly dull moment of our lives if we simply ask ourselves, "What am I doing right now?" In many Buddhist cultures, a bell is rung periodically throughout the day, as a way to draw attention back to the present moment. We can do this for ourselves in our own lives. We can ring a bell. We can set periodic reminders on our phones, put written signs around our homes and workspaces, or use any other reminder as a bell to draw our attention back to the present moment. This is the practice of observation, to constantly bring our awareness back to the present moment, time and time again.

At about four years old, my son had a habit of constantly putting his index finger in his mouth. We'd been to the dentist recently, and thankfully, the finger sucking hadn't caused any dental issues. I wanted to help him break this habit so that it wouldn't become a dental problem, as well as to prevent frequent occurrences of illnesses caused by him unknowingly putting germs into his mouth.

I began by explaining to my son in simple terms he could understand why it could potentially be harmful for him to continue sucking his finger. I told him that I noticed he tended to do it when he appeared bored or there wasn't anything particularly exciting going on. What was once perhaps a calming technique for him when he was an infant had turned into a mindless habit. I challenged him to try to notice every time he put his finger in his mouth or was about to put his finger in his mouth. When he noticed what he was doing, I encouraged him to say to himself, "I just put my finger in my mouth." I told him that once he noticed what he was doing and acknowledged it to himself he could then decide what he wanted to do. He could choose to keep his finger in his mouth, knowing the possible complications caused by finger sucking, or he could take his finger out of his mouth.

The first few times he put his finger in his mouth, I would nonchalantly say, "I just put my finger in my mouth." His eyes would get big as he noticed his behavior, then he would immediately pull his finger out of his mouth. After half a day of me being the observer for him, he began to notice his own behavior. He'd start to put his finger in his mouth, then declare, "I just put my finger in my mouth," and pull his finger away. At one point, he had his finger in his mouth; then upon realizing what had happened, he left his finger in his mouth and shouted, "Mommy, my finger is in my mouth. What do I do now?"

To which, I smiled and replied, "That's up to you."

He stopped sucking his finger within three days— a habit he had had since infancy gone in three days with the power of observation. By teaching him to observe his own behaviors and make his own decisions about his behavior, he not only became more aware of his habitual patterns but had agency in his decision-making about his behavior. The power of awareness is incredibly valuable. By resisting the trance of default mode and actively engaging in our lives, we gain insight and agency.

Within praise and shame societies, people are praised for "doing it all." The exhausted mother of young children who also works outside the home, who comes home and is fully engaged with her partner and children, and makes a homemade meal every night; the person who accepts extra responsibilities at work even when their workload becomes unbearable; the person who always extends their help to others even when they are drained; the person who never says no to get-togethers, immediately answers every text message and phone call, and regularly tends to their social media accounts. We emphasize the importance of being readily available at any moment. We want to appear as if we are always feeling great, always ready for action. We give and receive praise for appearing to lead idealized lives and find ourselves unhappy as we strive for what is unobtainable.

We've only recently acknowledged as a society the negative impacts that unskillful consumption of social media and constant availability can have on our mental health. Contrary to what our amygdalas may lead us to believe, we don't have to immediately respond to every text message; we have the choice whether or not to answer a phone call, and we don't have to attend every social outing. Sometimes by doing less, we are actually doing more.

Awareness of our thoughts and behaviors requires a moment of pause. I've been practicing as a nurse for eleven years, mostly in the inpatient pediatric and neonatal world. The best piece of advice I'd ever been given and therefore continue to spread to new practicing nurses is this: when you are so overwhelmed with tasks that you aren't thinking clearly, you need to *pause*. We can only skillfully handle a limited amount of sensory input before we start making mistakes because we lose the capacity to be mindful or intentional with our actions. It is apparent why working mindfully in the healthcare profession is imperative—because the lives of individuals are in their hands. If we ignore our brain's red flashing alarm bells screaming at us to slow down, we can make mistakes that can literally cost lives.

We are often overwhelmed by our tasks and responsibilities, and we fall into the trap of reacting mindlessly instead of responding mindfully. Reactivity is like touching a hot stove; it doesn't require higher level processing to make a decision about what to do next. The problem with reactivity, however, is that we don't give ourselves time to incorporate important details in our decisions. As an employee, we are more likely to make mistakes when we're moving too fast. As a parent, we are more likely to lose our temper and yell at our children when our nervous system is on fire. As a partner, we are more likely to say hurtful things when we feel hurt. In these scenarios of reactivity, we are not the only ones who could suffer the consequences of our lack of awareness and mindful action.

Responsiveness, on the other hand, requires careful observation of our internal and external environment, assessment of the situation, and conscious action. When we are responsive, as opposed to reactive, we are much more likely to reach desirable outcomes. Workplace responsiveness may entail making well-informed actions based on all the information we have. Responsiveness to a young child's display of anger may materialize as maintaining a calm presence, allowing a safe space for the emotions to move through. Responsiveness to conflict in a romantic relationship could involve recognizing that anger is arising and expressing our need for a break until we can calmly return to the conversation.

Responsiveness requires us to be able to look not only externally but also internally to identify what is present for us. We are out of tune with our bodies, which is a tragedy, because our bodies often tell us what's happening inside. When we regularly correlate our emotions with our bodily sensations, we learn to interpret what our bodies are telling us. A bodily sensation can trigger us to make time to pause and to observe what's present in order to skillfully respond to our environment.

There is an old parable about an alarmed rider on a wild horse galloping through town. A passerby calls out, "Where are you going?"

The rider yells back, "I don't know. Wherever the horse goes!"

When we aren't aware of the emotions we are experiencing, we risk being taken over by them, letting those unnoticed emotions dictate our actions. Naming emotions is a tool that helps you be more responsive and less reactive. We are only able to name three emotions, usually anger, happiness, and sadness. These three don't adequately describe all the emotions we truly experience. Some other emotions we may feel include joy, excitement, appreciation, contentedness, awe, pride, amusement, hopelessness, nervousness, disgust, stress, fear, and frustration.

There is a lot we can gain by mapping out our emotions on our body. Throughout our day, we experience a whole range of emotions, and these emotions are expressed in our bodies. When we feel angry, we can bring awareness to the moment and pause and then take note of where and what we are feeling in our bodies. Perhaps it is tightening in the jaw or a furrowed brow. Anger might feel hot, and it might have a color. When we feel fear creeping in, we can again take note of where and what we feel in the body. Fear might manifest as tension in the shoulders or an upset stomach. Does it have a temperature? Does it have a color? Joy might feel like an opening or fluttering in our heart center. By bringing a moment of awareness to what we're experiencing on an emotional and physical level, we begin the process of honoring ourselves where we're at and living our lives more intentionally.

Mapping emotions on our body takes time and space, inquiry, and reflection. Our bodies are connected to our internal world and tell us about our internal landscape, even when we're not consciously aware of it. By bringing an awareness to what is happening in our physical bodies and what emotions we're experiencing at the time, we give ourselves agency in the ability to respond instead of being stuck in habitual reactivity.

Anger can be tricky, as it can mask other emotions such as fear. Fear tends to leave us feeling vulnerable, which our primitive brains recognize as a survival threat. If we have an aversion to fear, our bodies may process fear as anger. We may perceive anger as being less vulnerable and more in control. Anger can, however, lead to reacting instead of responding, landing us in a more vulnerable, less controlled place. Any time we let emotions blindly lead us, irrationality leads the show.

By slowing down and paying more attention to what our bodies and emotions tell us, we can be more engaged with our lives and experience each moment more authentically. We discover more space for understanding, self-compassion, and engagement. We are no longer hapless riders on the wild horse of emotion; we are agents of change and intentional action in our own lives.

When we bring moments of awareness to daily activities, we can catch ourselves in habitual patterns. We wake up to the cell phone alarm, take the phone to the bathroom with us, and check our social media accounts while we pee. We wait in the school pickup line for our children, where we check our emails on our phones. We sit down for lunch and note the flavors of the first and the second bite; then we get lost in thoughts about something someone said to us or what we're going to do when we're done eating. We converse with a loved one and think about what we're going to say next instead of being present with their words.

Each moment of awareness we have, each moment we break the cycle of reactivity, creates an opportunity—opportunity to put the phone down, drop the thoughts, and be present with what is happening here and now. We can cultivate a more loving presence and awareness in hundreds of moments in our day, when we'd otherwise be riding along in old habitual patterns. These tiny spaces let us rediscover our true selves—how we relate to the world and how we engage with it. We gain the opportunity to cultivate the curiosity of a beginner's mind. We gain the chance to make different choices, break habits, and direct our horse instead of letting it direct us. Observation is the platform for curiosity, wonderment, and awe so that we can participate in our lives in a more authentic, engaged manner.

****

Awareness Exercise:

1. Add a mindfulness of emotions meditation to your meditation practice.

    So many of us live disconnected from our emotions. Either we don't recognize them or we push the uncomfortable ones away for fear that they'll control us. But the truth is, when we reconnect with our emotions mindfully, we are reconnecting with our humanity, and we give ourselves agency in how we interact with the world.

Guided Mindfulness of Emotions Meditation:

Begin by finding a comfortable seated position—one that is upright and alert, yet comfortable. Allow the eyes to gently close or rest half open in a slight downward gaze.

Do a quick scan of your body from head to toe, noticing and releasing any signs of obvious tension. Relax the brow line, unclench the jaw, relax the shoulders, and soften the belly. Soften the heart as well, to receive whatever arises with kindness and compassion.

Begin to connect with your breath, wherever you most easily notice it. It may be the cool tingling sensation at the back of your throat on the inhale, a warmth on your upper lip on the exhale, or the rise and fall of your chest or belly. Allow the breath to be your anchor to the present moment. With each breath, see if you can bring calm and ease. Inhale calm and exhale ease.

If the breath is not a comfortable anchor for you, see if you can rest your awareness on the sensations of your whole body sitting here.

After a few breaths, you will no doubt notice that your mind has wandered. Whenever this happens, recognize this as a normal activity of the mind. Then, without judgment, kindly bring the attention back to your anchor.

After a couple of minutes of resting your attention on the breath (or anchor of choice), see if you can allow your awareness to expand to any thoughts or sensations that are arising. Let your mind be like the sky and any thoughts or sensations like passing clouds. Gently notice them as they arise and pass on by.

After a few moments, see if you can become aware of any emotions that may be present for you. Bring your kind attention to whatever's here, gently naming the emotion to yourself. Joy, joy; bored, bored; anxious, anxious; sad, sad; grateful, grateful. If you're not noticing any emotions or are unaware of what you're feeling, that's okay too.

Now bring your awareness to where this emotion manifests in your body. Is there a tightness, a heaviness, or an opening in the chest? Is there a twisting or formation of knots in the belly? Do you notice soft eyes or a gentle smile? See if you can pay attention to what's there without judging it or trying to change it. Simply notice it.

You can even say to yourself, "Oh, this is anger" or "Hello, joy."
You now might consider noticing if there's a contraction or expansion
in response to this emotion. Oftentimes when a difficult emotion
arises, we might notice a contraction, an aversion to feeling this
emotion. When we experience pleasant emotions, there's often an
expansion we can notice.

Notice if there are any stories attached to the emotion, such as "I
shouldn't feel this way."

Now notice how the physical sensations might be changing as you
bring your awareness to them and how the emotions might be
changing as well. Do they change at all or do they stay the same? Do
they become stronger? Do they dissolve?

Emotions are not fixed or permanent but are rather like passing clouds
or intermittent weather. You are not the clouds or the weather. You are
the vast, spacious sky.

If an emotion becomes too overwhelming or uncomfortable, kindly
shift your attention back to your breath or feel the sensations of your
feet on the ground. Find comfort in being grounded and safe in this
moment.

Any time you notice you've gotten caught up in a thought, zoom out
and return to your place as the sky. Gently notice the patterns of
weather— the thoughts, the sensations, the emotions. They are all
simply different types of weather.

For the last couple of minutes, see if you can bring even more loving
kindness to your moment-to-moment experience. Find comfort in
knowing that you are the sky.

Journal Exercises:

1. Keep track of your emotions:

   The purpose of this exercise is to provide insight into your recognition and awareness of your emotions.
   For two days, keep track of all the emotions you experience.
   Next to each emotion as it arises, add a tally mark. At the end of the two days, ask yourself the following reflections:
   1. Did the results surprise you at all? Why?
   2. Did you recognize less than five emotions? How can learning to name all of your emotions serve you?

2. Map your emotions in your body:

   The purpose of this exercise is to get you more in tune with what your body is telling you about your mental and emotional landscape. The more you are aware of what is present inside you, the more skillfully you can respond to uncomfortable situations. Draw or print an outline of a human body and collect a few different coloring tools. When you experience a strong emotion, notice the sensations in your body. Color all the parts of your body where the emotion is manifesting in one color; then create a legend and label that emotion. You can also add what kind of sensation you are feeling there (i.e., tightening, opening, hot). Continue to map the emotions in your body until you've identified as many as you can. Refer to your body of emotions often until you can identify what emotions are arising based on the sensations in your body.

Chapter 4: Curiosity

We never cease to stand like curious children before the great mystery into which we were born.

—Albert Einstein

Spring is in the air, soil, and water. Carrot, cabbage, and cauliflower seeds nourish themselves in the fertile soil and swell with water, boldly preparing for transformation. Bright tulips beneath the magnolia tree coax her buds to bloom. "Just a little more rest," she pleads, her buds still enjoying their long nap. She knows she must awaken once again and wonders, "What will this season bring?"

Small, plastic pastel eggs hide discreetly in nature's vivid display of color. Jack runs wildly around the yard, Easter basket in hand, discovering joy in the journey. Everly's eyes fill with wonder, staring at the shiny, red plastic egg beside the red tulips. The juxtaposition sparks fascination and bewilderment in her beginner's mind. She meets Daddy's eyes, sharing the tenderness of the moment. The children fill their baskets with possibilities until they feel satisfied; then we sit and discover the surprises the tiny vessels hold.

I notice gratitude arising, a swelling of my heart, and a smile on my lips. Recognizing emotions requires attention and practice, and I'm expanding my awareness of all that is present. I let this joyful moment fill me up.

My mother-in-law tends the garden, watering freshly planted seeds. I imagine the seeds sighing with relief and delight as they drink the water. The seedlings continue to take refuge indoors under her gentle nurturing, and I jokingly tell her she is a NICU nurse. I admire her gardener's skill with plants, because I am not so skilled. When Alex and I first moved in together years ago, we discovered our desire for live house plants could not sustain them. Our futile efforts to keep any plant alive became a running joke. I was always first to pronounce a death, while he'd still be in adamant denial. I hated that he wouldn't acknowledge those losses. Denial is how he has addressed many of our problems.

Zen master Thich Nhat Hanh names a layer of our minds as "store consciousness," similar to the Western "subconscious." Inside our store consciousness lies wholesome and unwholesome seeds. Mindful actions water the wholesome seeds, such as love, peace, patience, and understanding. Mindless actions can water the seeds of hatred, anger, impatience, and delusion. Conscious choice and unconscious reaction yield gardens that are beautiful and bountiful or desolate and poisonous, respectively.

I contemplate the seeds I've been watering as a mother. Last night, I yelled at Jack after he demanded cookies for dinner and hit me, watering the seeds of anger and reactivity. His angry and sometimes physical outbursts have become more frequent since the pandemic began. Children have also suffered psychological distress due to COVID.

I should have handled that better. I'm a bad mother.

I breathe deeply and focus on physical sensations. I notice a heavy chest, a furrowed brow, and slumped shoulders.

Hello, Shame, I see you there.

I focus on the physical sensations and drop the bad mother narrative. I now use my breath as an anchor when I spiral into negativity or distraction. After a few minutes, I notice the physical sensations have disappeared, and I feel more relaxed.

I now consider the wholesome seeds I've watered. Immediately after yelling at Jack, I realized my mistake and apologized. I explained that Mommy felt frustrated and worried about him and that my emotions turned to anger because I didn't take care of them. I apologized for scaring him and told him that next time I felt frustration or worry I would take a few deep breaths or take a minute to myself so that I don't end up yelling. In doing this, I'd watered the seeds of humility and compassion.

This wasn't modeled for me as a child; there was very little accountability for adults' actions. I had vowed to myself, at a young age, to always make sure my future children knew I was sorry when I made a mistake. Unlike what I was taught as a child, respect is *not* to be *earned*; it is *inherent*. I want my children to know that I respect them, that their needs are just as important as mine, and that they are worthy of love and belonging just as they are.

Maybe, just maybe, I'm not a bad mother.

Every day, I water seeds in my children and myself. Like a gardener watering her future plants, our actions water our future happiness.

Let's hope my skills in nurturing wholesome store consciousness seeds beat my gardening skills.

Chocolate wrappers lie scattered across the patio, the evidence of their undoing on the faces of my children.

"Who said you could eat all that chocolate?" I facetiously ask them.

Jack offers Everly a mischievous grin and cackles, and she smiles like she's in on the joke. I love the way she looks at her brother. There is so much love in those eyes. I turn toward Alex, longing to share the moment with him, but he's not really here anymore. His vacant stare reveals his abandonment of the present, and I know exactly where he's gone. Anger immediately arises inside me, and before I've recognized what's present, I snap at him.

"I'm sorry if being here isn't interesting enough." The sarcastic words taste bitter as they leave my mouth, and I immediately wish I could suck them back out of the air, but they've already escaped.

He stares at me with a confused look on his face.

"I don't know what you're talking about. I'm fine," he deflects.

Here he goes again, denying the plant is dead.

"Whatever."

I shake my head, mad at him for checking out and mad at myself for letting my anger out. It takes time to recognize anger, and now it has escaped into hurtful words I can't reclaim. Finding and using the space between stimulus and response is difficult. As I see my anger, I know fear probably lurks behind, telling me I'm unworthy of love, unworthy of his attention. But in this moment, I still only feel anger.

"Do you all want to go for a walk?" I ask, hoping that maybe a change of scenery will bring us together again.

Alex and I secure the children in the stroller, and we begin our walk around the neighborhood. I share with him how this became a ritual for us when he was gone and ask if he'd be interested in listening to the Secular Buddhism podcast while we walk. To my delight, he agrees.

Three Approaches to Doubt and Mistrust, the newest episode, plays as we meander around together aimlessly. Noah begins the episode by quoting Korean Zen master Nine Mountain, "Small doubt, small enlightenment; big doubt, big enlightenment." Alex looks at me and playfully asks if I'm a Buddha yet, since I doubt everything. I laugh.

We had met in nursing school, so many of our early dates consisted of studying pathologies and diseases. We weren't the best study partners, because Alex would get frustrated when I wouldn't accept a claim as truth until I understood why.

"But why?" I'd ask him.

"Because the book and teacher say so," he'd respond.

That answer was never good enough for me. I would playfully remind him how we were taught that Pluto was a planet as children, and apparently that was wrong. I would rhetorically challenge him; if the educators were wrong about Pluto, what else were they wrong about? I would satirically amuse him with the "Pluto lie" as my reason for doubting.

Noah emphasized the importance of doubting our own views when on the path to liberating ourselves from our narrow views and seeing things as they truly are. We tend to scrutinize other peoples' perceptions and regard our claims as the only truth. He suggested we practice following news stories presented to our opposing political party. If we identify as a Democrat, we should listen to the news that Republicans are hearing and notice what is arising in us. If what arises is doubt or mistrust, we should then aim that toward our own personal view.

"Do you want to try it together?" I ask Alex, who is understandably reluctant at first.

Some of his patients in the hospital had previously denied the existence of COVID and hadn't practiced social distancing, and they lacked trust in the healthcare system. He'd expressed frustration to me about caring for these patients. Their reckless behavior had landed them in the hospital, and now he had to risk his own health to provide care to them while they told him how to do his job. One of his most recent patients said they had heard in the news that Vitamin C could cure the virus, so why weren't the hospitals trying that?

We discuss how the pandemic has turned into a political issue, the division between the two parties more polarized than we've ever experienced. I admit I've made harsh judgments and assumptions of Republicans, as if they all have identical characteristics.

We watch Republican news coverage, at Noah's suggestion, and realize Republican news and Democratic news have one major thing in common: Fear. The Democratic news stations warn us that an infection could kill us, that we should sanitize our groceries, stay home, and stay at least six feet from a person outside our household. The Republican news stations warn us that our freedom is threatened, that healthcare professionals lie about how deadly the virus is, and that the government keeps us from family, friends, and schools.

Having seen the effects of the virus with our own eyes in the hospital, we definitely mistrust the Republican stories about the "exaggerated" virulence of COVID. When we think about their claims of lost rights, we both notice doubt and frustration arising. Being nurses, we understand why we need to wear masks, and we've never felt it was a loss of our rights.

We attempt to turn around that doubt back on the news we're receiving. We can imagine what it might feel like to doubt it. Perhaps the push to sanitize our groceries and mail is a ploy to inspire fear. Maybe social distancing and mask wearing isn't necessary around people who aren't showing symptoms. Compassion arises inside me for this group I have "othered," as I realize the common humanity we share. I feel slightly more open-minded, more flexible with my idea of the truth. I vow to continue to ask myself, "Am I sure?"

"Are you okay?" I ask Alex, noticing he's gone quiet.

"I can't do this anymore," he pleads, this wound still too fresh. I gently squeeze his hand.

Curiosity bubbles up out of the stroller, the children wanting to stop and marvel at the neighbor's vibrant orange and pink perennials, the fragrant lavender bushes, and the golden yellow daffodils. Their noses jostle with the bees for the possession of the flowers. Witnessing my children's interactions with the world around them never ceases to amaze me.

"Ducks!" Jack squeals, pointing at the middle of the street.

Nine little ducklings follow Momma duck across the street. We walk slowly beside them, admiring the new family in our neighborhood. New season bringing new life. This season is calling us to be present, to slow down, and to be curious.

Back at home, we lay Everly down for her afternoon nap. Jack pleads for the camera again, photography being a new hobby. My phone's gallery is flooded with pictures of his Legos, his feet, his sister, and unflattering images of me and Alex. At the end of the day before I go to sleep, I scroll through my gallery to see the world through his eyes. It always brings a smile to my face.

I curl up on the couch, giving myself time with my thoughts. I still feel guilty for yelling at Jack last night but recognize the growth I've made. I was able to quickly notice I'd been reactive, whereas realization had taken longer before that. I'm slowly getting closer to finding the space between stimulus and response. By helping myself discover that space, I can teach my son that as well.

When I grow, my children grow.

Jack groans in frustration, disappointed at the image he has captured. He complains he can't see the tires of his toy truck.

"You just need to zoom out, buddy," Alex says as he kneels down beside him.

I admire Alex as he teaches Jack how to zoom in and zoom out with the camera. He explains that if he can't see the whole picture, he just needs to zoom out.

You just need to zoom out.

I contemplate on what I'm not seeing clearly, what I need to zoom out on. Ever since the birth of my first child, I have been plagued with the fear of "failing" as a mother, of not measuring up to my idea of a good mother.

Maybe I need to zoom out a bit.

I'm quite skilled at focusing on my mistakes, on the unwholesome seeds I water in myself and my children. Zooming out a bit, I realize that I also water wholesome seeds, seeds of humility, compassion, and kindness. Zooming out even further, I challenge my idea of what a "good mother" even is, whether it is fixed and definable. I reflect on all the things that have made me "me" and if "I" really can "be" anything at all.

Though sometimes I'd like to, I can't separate "myself" from all the things that have made me, me. I am my mother and father.

They are, and so I am *their* parents. I am the cities and cultures I have lived in. I am all the teachers who have taught me. I am my successes and failures. I am all of these and none of these.

Who am I? Can a label define me? Am I certain of all the things I hold as truths?

I am a baby bird, being thrown out of its nest. I feel the groundlessness my questioning prompts, but I don't feel afraid. I feel liberated. The lightness my doubts bring follows me through the rest of the day. There is an invigorating freshness to each, seemingly dull moment.

Alex and I are facing each other on the couch, exhausted after a busy day, trying to summon the energy for a meaningful connection. More often than not, at the end of the day, the first thing I think when I look at him is, "I haven't seen you yet today." Ever since I have had kids, I don't *see him* anymore. I see an extra set of hands to grab the diaper bag and snacks, to put shoes on squirmy feet, and to help me put out the daily fires.

"I'm sorry for what I said earlier when you checked out," I confess.

"I'm sorry for checking out," he says sincerely.

Here we both are, propelled by our habitual energies. He withdraws, I snap. But I feel a renewed sense of hope.

I just need to water the seeds of patience and compassion.

The Buddhist path suggests we should start with self-compassion; then we can more easily be compassionate toward others. It seems simple enough, but I struggle.

If it starts with self-compassion, I've got a long road ahead of me.

****

A year passes by. COVID vaccines have been developed and released to the public. Healthcare professionals have been among the first to receive the vaccine. The joy and relief we feel is short-lived, however, as other strains show up and people still get really sick.

I've continued my journey of waking up, observing myself and the world with nonjudgmental awareness. I can see my patterns of thought and behavior more clearly, yet I still struggle with self-compassion and my attachment to the idea of being a "good mom." I've plunged head first into Secular Buddhism and joined a sangha (a community of people that practice Buddhist principles together) in the Secular Buddhism podcast community. I have more awareness and engagement. I'm learning that liberating myself from suffering will be a lifelong effort.

Alex has begun his own journey. He began EMDR, a psychotherapy that is designed to help with past trauma. I'm slowly starting to see him wake up, too, and be more present when we're together. But he still carries a storm cloud with him, which threatens to bring him down and pull him away at any moment. He is still working in the ICU, caring for COVID patients. I see him suffering, yet try to be patient as he works things out in therapy. And I know somewhere, deep down inside of him, he knows he should leave the ICU. He knows he needs a break.

The kids are in bed, and the two of us are alone together.

Maybe this is a good time to ask him again.

"How has the job hunt been going?" I ask, doing my best to sound nonchalant.

"I haven't really checked the past few days," he admits.

"Why not?"

I suspect he's upset I've brought it up again, but I worry if I don't keep pushing, he'll stay stuck in this position forever, torturing himself. And we'll all be dragged along in his suffering.

"I don't know. Nothing looks that interesting. And…" he holds back.

"And what?" I ask.

"And leaving the ICU would feel like failing, like a step backward. I've worked so hard to get here," he explains.

I pause and breathe to allow space for processing the frustration arising so I can respond instead of reacting.

"Alex, what do you like about your job?"

"I'm good at it," he says.

"What else?" I push.

"I've worked so hard to get here," he says.

"Yeah, you said that before," I point out. "And yes, you are good at it."

He *is* good at his job. He has held many nursing leadership roles and brings experience, expertise, and wisdom with him. But that's not what I have asked, and I see he has avoided the question.

"Do you think you're still an ICU nurse because you *like* being an ICU nurse, or do you think your judgment is clouded by the time and energy you've invested into the role?"

His internal anguish is manifesting as physical discomfort, as he gets up and begins pacing the room.

"I don't know!" he says defensively.

I try to calm him down by lowering my voice.

"Honey, I think there are parts of you that enjoy being an ICU nurse. But to be honest, I feel like I'm witnessing my husband suffer in a job that causes him severe emotional distress," I say.

"I mean, there are some things I like about being an ICU nurse," he maintains. "I like knowing that I'm helping people when they're at their sickest, their most vulnerable."

I ask him to sit down, but he says he can't. He's too upset.

"Do you think a part of you is still an ICU nurse because you like being able to say, 'I'm an ICU nurse?'" I ask.

"Maybe," he grumbles.

"Ask me what I like about my job," I demand.

He complies.

"I love taking care of babies, and I love taking care of their parents. I enjoy teaching them how to safely care for their child. I love instilling confidence in them when it's time for their baby to be discharged and they're nervous about leaving," I proclaim sincerely.

He pauses for a moment, his face displaying anguish.

"I don't know anymore." His voice rises. "Sometimes I like it, but other times, I have no idea why I'm doing it anymore. I'm not oblivious to how it's affecting me. I have nightmares all the time. I can't even be present with my family because I continually replay the depressing shit I see. I'm not happy," he admits.

"You aren't stuck," I remind him. "You can leave. You can still take care of people in a different way, without sacrificing your own happiness."

"A part of me knows you're right, and I'm so tired of being unhappy, but I can't just walk away. I can't!" he declares.

"Yes, you can. You matter. Your life matters. Your happiness matters. You've given over ten years of yourself to this role. It's okay to take a break. It's okay to choose your happiness," I stress.

"Okay, fine, I do want to stop, I do! I just don't think I can walk away from it. Sometimes I wish I'd make a mistake, and they'd have to let me go!"

His words linger in the air, piercing our hearts. My heart bleeds for him.

You just need to zoom out, dear one.

****

Instead of approaching each situation with curiosity, we often think to ourselves, "I've been here before. I know how this will go." We forget to look for the beauty and the uniqueness in each moment, and because of this, we miss out on a lot. We make assumptions that lead to unskillful actions.

I love remembering how my daughter at six months old, sitting in the grass in our backyard, was in awe of everything around her. She took careful notice of each hand and each finger. She was intrigued by the feel of the blades of grass in her hands and took time to inspect a single blade. She marveled at every detail in her surroundings: the bugs, the plants, her body, the light. Everything was new, and everything was her teacher. She was a student, learning about the world.

We all enter the world this way, with a beginner's mind. We are not born with a mental framework of how the world "works." That framework is learned. We are born without knowledge, without biases, without shame. We acquire knowledge from our experiences, we absorb biases from our culture and upbringing, and we develop shame from fear of rejection and isolation. In our early years, however, we learn in such a unique way because we see things as they actually are. We do not yet have anything to compare these new experiences to; each experience is unique. We look at things without judgment, because we have no framework yet with which to compare things to. This flower is not more or less pretty than that flower; they are just two different flowers.

As we get older, we develop frameworks of everything we've experienced in our lives. These mental frameworks are built up of patterns we've noticed and help us to navigate our way through our lives. These patterns include concepts and symbols and our perception or interpretation of them. Some of our mental frameworks include confirmation bias, by which we interpret information to confirm what we already believe, and fundamental attribution error, by which we blame certain human behavior on individual character traits rather than the situation.

These mental frameworks make it easier and more convenient for us to navigate through our daily lives. Not much feels completely new to us, because every new experience we encounter we try to fit into one of our previously developed mental models. By doing this, we create assumptions and expectations of every situation we encounter. This allows us to move through our day more efficiently, but not necessarily more effectively or more mindfully.

We've all experienced moving through life this way, which is akin to a hamster running on a wheel. The hamster has the pattern memorized—how far to stretch its legs to reach the next wheel spoke and how fast to move its legs to keep up with the pace of the wheel. The pattern becomes an internal mental model for them that they no longer need to focus on in order to complete the task; they just keep on running. We are often very much like a hamster on a hamster wheel, moving on autopilot, going through the motions of our lives without taking notice of our surroundings or even realizing that we're on a hamster wheel at all.

If you've ever been driving a vehicle and spaced out for a while only to find yourself at the wrong destination, one that you've driven to often but didn't intend to drive to that day, you've been under the influence of your mental framework. In this situation, your brain was working on autopilot, using old mental frameworks to navigate you to your destination, which allowed other parts of your brain to be distracted.

We often operate throughout the majority of our day in this checked-out, autopilot mode, where we are less aware of our surroundings, our environment, the people around us, and ourselves. Just like the hamster, we have the option at any point of hopping off the hamster wheel and looking around us. The first step is recognizing that we are on a hamster wheel. Unfortunately, a lot of us don't recognize when we're living our lives half asleep, much less engaged, much less curious about the world around us. We've more or less told ourselves that we are the expert on all that we will encounter from now on, so there's no more need for curiosity.

There are, of course, many important situations that require us to rely on and trust our expertise in a subject area. We do ourselves a great disservice, however, when we tell ourselves we've seen it all, and there's nothing new to learn. We stunt our own individual growth by carrying an all-knowing attitude. Assumptions about others and the way things work in the world on a small scale can lead to our own individual suffering, and on a large scale, it can lead to prejudice, social injustice, and the destruction of our planet and all things living on it. When we hold on tightly to and give merit to beliefs such as these groups of people are this way, or all people who have this belief behave that way, we limit ourselves. We limit our ability to develop deep compassion, we limit our ability to understand the truth, and we limit our ability to let go of old, stale beliefs.

Human understanding of the world and the way everything works is always changing. There have been countless times throughout history that we believed we had discovered an ultimate truth, only to later discover that we were wrong. We've all had to adjust our own mental frameworks based on new information that has been presented to us. Many of us as children were taught in school that Pluto was a planet, and we accepted that as truth, only to have the International Astronomical Union (IAU) change its classification to a dwarf planet in 2006. It was also once widely accepted that Christopher Colombus discovered America and that he offered compassion and shelter to the Native Americans; however, we've come to learn that America was not first discovered by Columbus and that he committed genocide against Native Americans.

When we are presented with new information that conflicts with our current set of beliefs and mental frameworks, we experience cognitive dissonance. This psychological phenomenon is characterized by a sense of discomfort that we feel when we hold two ideas or beliefs that conflict with each other. If a woman who identifies as pro-life becomes pregnant and chooses to not keep the baby, she will likely experience cognitive dissonance. Someone who comes out as gay may experience cognitive dissonance if they were raised with oppressive views about sexual orientation. Once these mental frameworks we've spent so many years developing become challenged, we struggle to cope with the dissonance we experience.

About a year and a half ago, I had been spending a great deal of time thinking about compassion for others. I'd read a few stories about Buddhist monks who believe in reducing suffering for all living creatures, including insects. Some of these stories included monks, who while cleaning the monastery would avoid stepping on or washing away insects. These stories described compassion as a seed that could be cultivated; in that, if you water it, it will grow.

Around the same time I was contemplating compassion for others, I began to question my eating habits, specifically with regard to eating animals. I'd heard of the studies about animal agriculture's negative impact on climate change, which I considered myself to be passionate about. I had already switched from disposable to reusable grocery bags and paper towels to reusable rags, and I'd begun composting my food scraps and generally made choices that were supporting my value of reducing my negative impact on climate change.

When it came to making changes to my food choices, however, that was something that took a long time for me to wrap my head around. What we eat is largely influenced by our culture and tradition. We tend to gravitate toward foods we grew up eating and have attitudes toward food similar to what we grew up with. Whether we grow up eating vegetarian, omnivorous, halal, or anything else, our ideas about food are influenced by our culture. We have mental frameworks about what is good to eat and what is not good to eat. Challenging our mental framework of a good diet can be incredibly confusing and distressing.

When I began to conceptualize and acknowledge the impact my diet had on the environment, I was thrown into an uncomfortable state of cognitive dissonance. I recognized that my actions (eating animal products) did not align with my values (importance of reducing our negative impact on the environment). The more I read about animal agriculture's impact on the environment, the more conviction I felt for giving up animal products altogether. It also led me to feeling like the rug had been swept out from underneath my feet, like my understanding of the world had just changed; it was incredibly uncomfortable. Nothing in the world changed at this moment, just my perception and interpretation of it.

After thoughtful deliberation, I decided to switch to a plant-based diet. What largely started as a means to reduce my environmental impact became an exercise of compassion. I began to look at all animals differently. When taking my children to the petting zoo and petting a cow, I would think about how less cows would suffer because of my choices. When reading books about farm animals, I began to wonder about the personalities of each individual pig and chicken. By aligning my actions with my values, I was also watering seeds of compassion.

We can be very passionate about the beliefs we have about the world. Things we once thought we knew to be true can be challenged. The discomfort we feel when our ideas are challenged, however, is caused by us. Suffering doesn't naturally exist when ideas change; that is something we as human beings add to the situation. Becoming more aware and educating ourselves in itself doesn't cause suffering and discomfort. We experience suffering because we have told ourselves that our beliefs were the absolute truth, but we told ourselves a lie.

Nothing is for certain. No idea or belief is immune to speculation or interrogation. Since nothing is for certain and our beliefs are subject to conjecture, the most skillful approach we can take is to loosen our grip on our beliefs. Instead of saying to ourselves, "I know this to be true," we should instead say to ourselves, "I believe this to be true with the information I have processed at this time, but I am flexible and open to new ideas." Imagine if we had this type of relationship with our beliefs and what that would mean for our well-being when one of our current beliefs was shattered by new knowledge. We would integrate the new knowledge into our mental frameworks and move on; we would not experience the suffering that comes from our own rigid thinking. Our relationship with our beliefs and our ideas of the truth is a fundamental practice to cultivating a mind that is curious and open to learning new things.

We tend to put a lot of emphasis and praise on knowledge and shy away from uncertainty and doubt. We dress ourselves up in our credentials, our labels, our accomplishments and hide our confusion and ignorance. It can be scary to acknowledge what we don't know for sure, or even whether we can know *anything* for sure. Cultural influences and biological processes drive us toward striving for certainty. Our survival brain wants to be able to explain everything, to label everything, and to have an answer to everything. Our survival brain feels threatened when it is experiencing uncertainty. Ambiguity and skepticism can cast us out of equilibrium, where we feel comfortable and safe. We want to believe that we have a firm foundation and that everything we hold on to tightly is keeping us safe. We are drawn to the illusion that one day we will have all the answers and that somehow answers to everything will solve our pain and suffering.

This false assurance we give ourselves causes us to suffer further. We deceive ourselves when we tell ourselves that answers and knowledge have the ability to cease all suffering. Nothing is immune to change or skepticism. The nature of impermanence and interdependence is such that everything is constantly evolving and everything is interacting to and responding to everything else in the environment. This means that truths are impermanent too.

Most of us have heard the expression, "You can't step in the same river twice." This expression illuminates the nature of impermanence and interdependence. What we consider to be "the river" is actually a moving, changing, different thing each moment. The water that flows through is never the same water as before; the flowing water moves small pebbles downstream; animals move through the river and take the nutrients they need; plants grow, die, and return to the soil. When we say "the river," it is skillful to acknowledge it as something different today from what it was yesterday.

The truth is, we are never done with our work of learning about ourselves, others, and the world around us. We are always changing, and the world is always changing. Everything is in a constant state of change, and if we close our eyes too long, we will wake up one day and not realize how we got here.

The key here is to stop striving to be the expert at everything, to admit to ourselves that maybe we don't know. We can open the blinds to our mind and let the light in and be curious about what we see and about what we might still not be seeing.

Shunryu Suzuki Roshi, Soto Zen monk, who helped popularize Zen Buddhism in the United States said, "In the beginner's mind there are many possibilities. In the expert's mind there are few." This is known as shoshin. Shoshin describes a mind that is curious, liberated from concepts and notions, open and free to explore different possibilities.

There are many ways we can cultivate shoshin. They all begin with entering into a state of observation. We can do this through formal meditation or mindfulness practices. We can simply ask ourselves, "What is happening right now? What is happening inside my body? What is happening around me?" Awareness is the key to a beginner's mind, to cultivating space for curiosity to grow.

When we're strengthening our attention to the present moment, knowing why something is the way it is, is much less important than just acknowledging that things are the way they are. For example, if we are observing sensations in our body and notice tension in our jaw or anywhere else in the body, we can simply notice it and then release the tension. When we bring awareness to our mind, we can recognize any thoughts or emotions without judgment and then notice when they float away. We can notice our role in our perception of our environment, as far as what we are adding to it. What beliefs and judgments, what stories, what preconceived notions do we have that are altering our perception of our surroundings? Oftentimes this distinction can be difficult to make because we tend to really believe that the stories we've created in our heads are objective truths, but they rarely, if ever, are. Again, the question here is what, not why.

There is an old Buddhist parable about six blind men and an elephant. The story goes that six blind men each touched a different part of an elephant, attempting to describe what an elephant was from their individual point of view. The first man, touching the elephant's side, described the animal as a wall. The second, touching the tusk, was adamant that the animal was like a spear. The third, touching the trunk, declared the animal to be like a snake. The fourth, touching the leg, exclaimed the animal was like a tree. The fifth, touching the ear, announced the animal was like a fan. Finally, the sixth man, feeling the tail, stated the elephant was like a rope. They quarreled over who was right, when in truth they were all partially right and all a little wrong.

We are all blind men touching an elephant, with our life experiences, our judgments, and our beliefs altering our view of reality. Although we may never be able to truly and successfully rid ourselves of all of our preconceived notions and ideas, we can acknowledge that we have them. By acknowledging the existence of the filters through which we personally see the world, we cultivate shoshin.

In each moment of awareness and acute observation, the next thing we should ask ourselves is, "What is my practice in this situation?" If we notice that thoughts are rushing in, our practice is to gently notice them and watch them recede into the waves. If we observe emotions, we observe their effect on our bodies and, without clinging or pushing away, gently notice as they melt away. Each time we do this, we burst open a space of possibility.

What can we create when we don't limit ourselves to our own individual version of the truth? What possibilities exist when we are boundless, unattached to our perceptions and labels? What world exists outside of our stories? Each moment as it arises is an opportunity—an opportunity to hop off the hamster wheel and take a look around us with curiosity.

There are times in our lives when we may feel "stuck"—stuck in an unhappy relationship, stuck in an unfulfilling job, stuck with some undesirable habits we're struggling to change. If we make space for observation and curiosity, we may discover alternative solutions, alternative ways of being that we hadn't noticed before. Some questions we can ask ourselves when we feel stuck are: Do I really know everything there is to know about this? How else can I look at this problem?

When we begin to explore all the possibilities of cultivating shoshin, it is normal to feel a bit overwhelmed at first. While it is exciting to realize that this hamster wheel is not the only option for us, fear and other uncomfortable emotions can also come up when we realize all the other truths, all the other paths. Are our actions in alignment with our values? Do our words, our actions match our highest selves? Realizing our actions are out of alignment with our core values is like having the rug swept out from under our feet. When we realize the ground we stand on isn't the firm foundation we once believed it to be, it can be very unnerving. Wisdom teaches us, however, that there never was a firm foundation; the only difference now is that we are aware of it and acknowledging it. Our job here is to practice self-compassion, to hold ourselves with a nonjudgmental, loving awareness.

****

Awareness Exercises:

1. Continue your daily meditation practice.

2. Practice doubting one of your personal views to grow your beginner's mind.

The purpose of this exercise is to inspire curiosity and compassion. By doubting things we consider to be the truth, we open ourselves up to other possibilities and compassion for people with opposing views. Begin by contemplating something you hold to be true, that others don't always agree with. Next, bring doubt and uncertainty to your view. Consider asking someone with this conflicting view how they experience their truth, while trying to imagine what it might feel like to think the same way.

Journal Exercise:

1. How rigid are your beliefs? You might explore this question by contemplating whether any of your beliefs have ever changed. If you have had a belief change, how tightly do you now hold on to this new belief?

Chapter 5: Self-Compassion

The whole cosmos has come together to produce us. We carry the whole world inside us. That is why, to accept yourself and love yourself is an expression of gratitude.

—Thich Nhat Hanh

The sky blankets us with thick clouds, overcast after the morning rain. The fresh scent of dew and daffodils emerges from the wet earth as she exhales with gratitude for this sustenance. Sparkling puddles entice my adventurous children to test their depths. Giggles and muddy water collide in the air as they play uninhibited.

Their quest for worms commences, as they turn over every brick in our garden. Everly leads the expedition, with her rainbow-colored boots poking out from the bottom of her shiny baby blue raincoat. Jack follows behind her, toting a bright red bucket to collect their specimens. I roll a brick over, revealing a big, fat, juicy worm wriggling in moist soil.

"Worm!" Everly shrieks with joy, pointing to our discovery.

I pick up the slimy pink worm and hand it to my eager daughter, as I do my best to disguise my disgust.

Don't pass on your irrational fears to your children.

Everly tenderly holds the wriggling worm in her hands, and we examine its translucent body. Jack offers his bucket of dirt as its new humble abode, and she gently places it inside. They continue meandering around the yard together until their bucket is full and their little boots and hands are muddy.

A herd of muddy boots trample into the house while I'm untying my shoelaces.

"Jack! Everly! Stop!" I yell angrily. "Look what you just did!"

Their worried eyes look down, then back up at me.

"Come take your boots off outside right now!" I demand.

While they take off their boots, I take a couple of deep breaths and do a quick body scan. The immediate sensations I notice are a tight jaw and furrowed brow.

Hello, Anger. I see you there.

I recognize judgmental thoughts creeping in, such as "I shouldn't feel this way" and "a good mother wouldn't feel angry." I gently bring my attention back to the physical sensations. I soften where I can and notice as the sensations slowly begin to fade. I invite curiosity into the space to discover what else is present. My muscles feel weak, my eyes heavy, and my energy low.

Aha, I'm tired. Hello, Fatigue.

My body needs rest to refill. Fatigue has drained my "bucket," leading me to be reactive instead of responsive.

"I'm sorry I yelled at you. Next time I want you to do something, I'll ask more kindly," I tell the kids. "I realized I am feeling tired."

I kiss their little foreheads and coax them to the couch. They've already had their allotted screen time today, but the only way for me to get rest is to let them exceed their hour-long limit.

Good moms ... can't be defined in one way. I don't know, with certainty, what a good mom is. I will feel better and be more patient and engaged if I let myself rest. I will model self-love for my children.

The three of us snuggle underneath the giant, fuzzy red blanket on the couch. I am fast asleep within a few minutes of the movie starting and awaken to a text message an hour later from Alex.

"I swear I'm cursed! Normal patient just stroked out on me!" he said.

"Oh man. So annoying. I hope it doesn't follow you to the surgery center!" I replied.

Alex is finishing his last week in the ICU before he starts his new job in an outpatient surgery center, where he will no longer be witnessing daily trauma. His decision to leave was very difficult, as his identity was so tightly bound to being an ICU nurse. It has been heart-wrenching to watch him grieve losing that title, and yet I also feel proud of him. He is learning to give to himself that same compassion he gives freely to his patients. We are both learning that self-compassion is not *selfish*.

"Mommy, I'm hungry! Get me a snack," Jack declares.

"Me too, Mommy. Get me food!" Everly agrees.

"I'm hungry, Mommy. Will you please make me a snack?" I suggest to them.

"Mommy, will you please make me a snack?" they repeat synchronously.

"Yes, I will," I reply, smiling at them.

I stand up and stretch my refreshed body, then go to the kitchen to prepare snacks for my children. I breathe in deeply, grounding myself in the present moment, and set the intention to be present with this otherwise mundane task. The Honeycrisp fashions red and yellow streaks and speckles like a risky painter has gotten ahold of it. The whoosh and thump of each slice through the apple creates a rhythmic anchor to the present moment. The sweet, fruity aroma arouses and captures my senses, causing my mouth to water. I delicately slice out the core, observing the artistic seed pattern. I'm surprised to discover how much joy I can experience by merely cutting an apple. I plate the apple slices and my mind drifts to self-judgment for snapping at the kids earlier.

I gently place my hand on my heart and close my eyes. I call on my RAIN practice, a mindfulness technique I learned from Tara Brach, a psychologist and Buddhist meditation teacher. I begin with the R of RAIN—*recognize*. Recognizing what emotion is present is easy as it's an emotion I've become very familiar with throughout my life.

I see you there, Shame. I know you're trying to protect me, but I'm OK.

The next step of RAIN is to *allow* the experience to be as it is. This step still feels dangerous to me. Instead of pushing away this uncomfortable emotion, I allow it to be as it is.

It's OK to come out from behind those shadows, Shame. You're welcome here.

I smile as she slowly approaches. Her head hangs low and her shoulders are slumped, crushed by gravity and blame that does not belong to her. As I extend my hand out to her, she reluctantly places her hand in mine, and I pull her into the light. She tries to hide it, but I see the weight of what she's carried her whole life in her sad eyes, her wounds. But I don't look away, even for a second. She is beautiful, radiant even, and I stand in awe as the light shines through all of her broken parts.

I move to the next step of RAIN, *investigate*, by asking with curiosity, "What is it that I am believing? What does this hurting part need most from me?" It's no surprise to me that I'm still believing that I'm a bad mother, that shame and self-judgment continue to debilitate me. I look deeply into this suffering, this shame, searching for what this part of me needs.

Reassurance. I need reassurance. And forgiveness.

I search deep inside for my most awakened self to *nurture* my wounds, the final step of RAIN. I find her standing alone in a grassy meadow. The sun highlights her gentle gaze and inviting smile, and she has a warm and accepting presence.

"You can forgive yourself for the mistakes you make, dear one. You are a good mother and a good person. You are worthy of forgiveness, love, and belonging," I whisper to myself.

I linger in this space of self-compassion for a moment, letting the comfort I am providing hold my body. I am both the holder and the one being held.

I return my attention to my breath. I rescan my body and notice the heaviness in my chest is gone and my shoulders are relaxed. Shame was present in my body but has passed through.

I watered seeds of reactivity earlier with my children, but then I watered seeds of humility and self-compassion.

I must often remind myself that mindfulness is a practice. Sometimes I catch myself before I become reactive, and sometimes it's smack dab in the middle of an ugly meltdown. It's like I have an alter ego who steps outside of me for a moment and says, "Hey, you're stuck in reactivity again. Come back into your body. Pause and breathe." I find myself mixed up with the same emotions, triggered by the same things, over and over again. So over and over again, I'm learning to bring loving awareness to myself in those moments. And sometimes it isn't even my alter ego who brings me back, who shines the light in the dark places. Sometimes it's my children.

Yesterday, I was in a frenzy getting Jack ready for school, slamming dresser drawers and snapping orders at him. Before I'd even become aware of the state I was in, Jack kindly looked at me and said, "Momma, it seems like you're feeling frustrated. Do you want me to take deep breaths with you?" Tears immediately filled my eyes, and I graciously accepted his offer. We sat on my bed breathing together, in silence.

I've even started noticing Jack show himself compassion. He'll scream in frustration when he accidentally breaks his newest Lego creation, then go to his room and begin taking slow deep breaths until he feels better.

I used to think giving myself love and compassion was excusing my bad behavior. I used to think it was self-indulgent. But direct experience has shown me my self-compassion practice produces less reactivity and encourages my family members to be compassionate. By showing myself love, I am also loving others.

Bringing awareness to how full my bucket is allows me to make skillful decisions. When my bucket is near empty, I'm surviving; I need rest, support, self-compassion, and understanding. Unrealistic expectations of myself prompt disappointment, frustration, and shame. When my bucket is near full, I'm thriving; I can extend help to others. I can look and reach for opportunities to grow. My work lies in my ability to recognize and honor where I'm at mentally and physically.

Today, my energy matches the weather—cloudy with intermittent showers. I find a break in my showers after the kids eat their snack, and we build a makeshift beach in the living room. Jack's mattress offers a cozy spot to rest on the "sand," and dark blue sheets on the floor offer the illusion of a sparkling blue ocean. Reggae plays in the background while we play with sand toys and throw the beach ball around.

Vivid memories of building large, multi room forts with my mother and siblings play in my head. Her vivacious and spirited nature made for a lot of fun during family games. Some of my childhood memories are like this; I try to remind myself of the pleasant times.

The sound of the garage door opening propels the children off the mattress.

"Daddy's home! Daddy!"

Alex bursts through the door and greets us enthusiastically, "Where are my kids? There are my kids! Where is my wife? There is my wife! Hi! Hi! Hi! I missed you!"

Jack and Everly giggle and jump in circles around him in their swimsuits, careful not to touch his germy scrubs.
"What is going on here?" Alex asks, laughing.

"We're at the beach, obviously," I reply jokingly.

"I want to join! Okay, Daddy's going to take a quick shower and join you guys," he tells them, and he kisses the tops of their heads before running to the basement shower.

Gratitude arises in my body, an opening heart space and a gentle smile. Over the past few months, I've witnessed Alex begin to wake up and return to us. He fills up more space in our home now, and we all feel his presence.

I'm so happy he's back.

I can appreciate how difficult this new practice of self-compassion has been for him. He's spent most of his life being a "yes" person. Can you do overtime? *Yes.* Can you take an extra patient even though you're slammed? *Yes.* Can you help me with my pain and suffering? Can you fix this problem? Can you put your needs aside for me? *Yes. Yes. Yes.*

He'd been faithful to the hamster wheel for so long that he was afraid to step off. What if he stops saying *yes*? Who will he be? Who will be there to say *yes* to the things he says no to?

Well aware of how scarce my bucket is and meeting myself with compassion, I decide to make it a "you pick dinner" night. These glorious nights grant me the permission to not worry myself sick over my kids not eating.

Dinosaur chicken nuggets roar and lose limbs as they engage in an epic battle as the kids play and eat. Alex recounts his absurdly traumatic day at work. I attempt to practice deep listening to hold space for him and his suffering but feel distracted by overwhelming gratitude that these painful exchanges will soon be far in the past.

"Oh, I forgot to tell you, Trevor and his family will be in town next month, and I wanted to see how you felt about inviting them to Jack's birthday," he mentions.

Well, there goes my stress-free dinner, damn it.

"Are they vaccinated?" I ask.

"Yeah … Well, he and his wife are. Their daughter obviously isn't," he says.

I freeze. A penne pasta noodle is hanging from my fork. I weigh all the risks and benefits. My best friend's daughter's birthday party had just passed. They had rented out an ice cream truck for her and invited the whole neighborhood block of children. Her daughter looked so happy.

I want Jack to experience a birthday party like that. I don't want him to miss out on special childhood experiences with friends. My kids deserve that kind of fun too… But what if I invite someone who has asymptomatic COVID and they get everyone sick? What if some guests get really sick and it's my fault because I was reckless?… I'm so fucking tired of being cautious… Wow, how bad does that make me sound?

"Heather?" a distant voice calls.

"Huh? Oh … sorry," I say, returning to my body. "Um. I don't know."

"What's your hesitation about?" he asks.

Parents have enough damn things to worry about. Make sure your children eat a healthy diet, but empower them to make their own choices. Protect them from predators (who seem to be everywhere now, according to the news), but don't shelter them so much that they can't enjoy autonomy or learn to protect themselves. Don't give them too much screen time but also consider that we live in a digital world. Earn enough money so you can live in a nice neighborhood in a good school district, but don't work so much that you aren't present with them. Parent them mindfully, without passing on your childhood trauma, even when you're exhausted from doing everything listed here. Oh and now, make sure they have a fulfilling, joyful childhood but try not to spread COVID and kill people.

Fear and guilt just circling around, darling.

We decide we'll ask our other at-risk birthday guests if they're comfortable with an out-of-state guest coming and delegate this moral conundrum to them. We're both so tired of making these decisions. For two years since the start of the pandemic, vaccines have been available, and we still worry about every social decision we make. We limit our interactions with others and feel sad our children are missing important early childhood experiences. We let our guard down by socializing with any other person and feel worried and guilty for potentially getting someone sick.

The kids snuggle together in bed while I read them a picture book about emotions before they go to sleep. The kids enjoy pausing on each page and describing how they experience that particular emotion. We get to the page about feeling shy, and Jack declares his unfamiliarity with that emotion. I laugh in agreement.

"You are a social butterfly, buddy," I tell him.

I turn the page and recognize the girl struggling to tie her shoelaces. That frustrated girl is me. In my daily experience with life, there are still so many struggles, even two years after the beginning of the pandemic and after starting a mindfulness practice. When I began this practice, I sought relief from my suffering but wasn't prepared for the complex ride that this practice has taken me on. Learning to open to experiences, positive and negative, has opened me to emotions that I wasn't aware of before. I feel more raw, more vulnerable than I did, and I'm learning to balance welcoming what's present with self-compassion. When I zoom out on my experience of the last couple of years, I see how far I've come. I'm much less reactive, much less judgmental of myself. It's still there, but it has softened. Recognizing this, I allow myself to be kind and accept this feeling of frustration.

This, too.

The kids are tucked into bed, and Alex and I are on the couch. He has been more open with me about his emotions lately, which is difficult for him. Every time he opens up to me about his pain and suffering, he apologizes for burdening me. And every time he apologizes, I tell him not to and promise him that helping him helps me.

He tells me how drained he feels, how depleted of energy and disconnected he feels, how powerless he feels. He sees the suffering of the world and wants to fix it all. He admits he recognizes now that he can't, but that's hard for him to accept. One person alone can't heal all the world's wounds, and certainly not from a place of scarcity. He's trying to save the world with an empty bucket. I'm familiar with the pain of that never-ending race, and I'm beginning to find my way out.

Maybe I can help him fill his bucket.

"I feel terrible, like I'm abandoning my coworkers. Like I'm bailing on them after all we've been through together," he says, referring to his transition to his new job.

He feels shame for not being what he thinks he should be. I know that feeling intimately.

"I'm so sorry you're carrying that weight. I don't think anyone will be mad at you or blame you for leaving, but I understand that it's hard for you to leave them," I say sincerely.

"None of us expected a pandemic to happen, but then it did. And we all got through it together. And now what? I have to just say goodbye to all these people I've been through literal hell with? Why do I get to just walk away?" he expresses, wearing guilt all over his face.

I let silence fill the room for a moment, resisting the urge to react unskillfully.

"Nothing can erase the work you did in those hospital rooms, with all those patients. Nothing can take away what you've been through with your coworkers. Nothing can—not even leaving. It's OK to choose yourself now, to choose your own healing now," I tell him.

His shoulders relax down away from his ears, and his posture becomes less stiff.

"I know you're right, that it's OK to leave and it doesn't make me a bad person. But deep down it just feels…" He shakes his head. "I'm sorry for complaining about this again. I'm sure you're probably tired of hearing me complain about it."

Don't you see, darling? Helping you fills my bucket.

****

When we bring more awareness to our thought and behavior patterns, we will likely discover that we constantly fall short of our personal expectations and values. Even if we dedicate hours to reducing our reactivity, we alternate between conscious responding and unconscious reacting. We desperately cling to things that we desire and push away anything that makes us uncomfortable. As we open to all experiences, both desirable and undesirable, we experience discomfort as we become more aware of our own shortcomings. A new mindfulness practice is like opening a closet door to things you've hidden away. Our work lies in our ability to stay open to these experiences, fully present and aware of what is happening inside and outside of our bodies. In order to maintain this practice, self-compassion is a critical component to our ability to stay open, nonjudgmental, and grow.

Uncomfortable emotions will likely arise when we first examine ourselves with these tools. Some can reveal the truth and further our growth, but others can cloud the truth, make us feel worthless, and hinder our growth. How we handle frustration and disappointment when we see a disconnect between our actions and our values determines whether or not this moment will advance our personal growth. When we approach the disconnect with judgment, shame degrades our power to change. Shame tends to be a default emotion for many of us when we've done something we're not proud of, because we haven't exercised self-compassion enough. As a child, we may have been told, "You shouldn't feel that way" or "suck it up." Instead of being coached on how to handle difficult emotions as they arose, we may have been silenced or shamed.

Shame can arise when we inspect our flaws and moral inconsistencies without loving awareness. Ironically, we tend to extend love and compassion to others more readily than ourselves. Brené Brown, a well-known public speaker and researcher on shame, describes shame as "… the intensely painful feeling or experience of believing that we are flawed and therefore unworthy of love, belonging, and connection" in her novel *Atlas of the Heart* (Brown

2012, 69). She differentiates shame from guilt by defining shame as a focus on self and guilt as a focus on behavior. This subtle distinction shifts our thought from "I am bad" to "I did something bad." Many of us were shamed when we made childhood mistakes and now self-shame when we've made an adult mistake, as an attempt to change our behavior.

Shame is a poor motivator for change, especially when endured over time. In a meta-analysis by Budiarto and Helmi, it was shown that shame has a negative correlation with self- esteem; as our shame increases, our self-esteem decreases (Budiarto and Helmi 2021, 131–45). If we frequently shame ourselves, we increasingly de-value ourselves and lose confidence in our ability to change. Low self-esteem indicates self-doubt in our ability to do better and lack of self- compassion.

Those unfamiliar with self-compassion may think, "Oh, self-compassion is not for me; that sounds selfish, and I will probably not achieve as much. I need to be hard on myself." However, psychological science says otherwise. The research of Dr. Kristin Neff shows that self-compassion motivates far better than shame (Neff 2023, 193–218). Self-compassion does not perpetuate complacency; it kindly acknowledges suffering as part of life and supports improvement.

It is also not the same as self-pity, by which we forget that other people in the world are experiencing the same suffering. Neff describes self-compassion as requiring three components: self-kindness (avoiding self-judgment and negative self-talk), common humanity (recognizing that others struggle just as we do), and mindfulness (the ability to be present and notice what is happening, as opposed to over identifying with the emotion) (Neff 2023, 193–218).

Self-compassion is the ability to hold our pain, flaws, and failures with kindness and understanding, with the intention of healing our wounds and improving ourselves. It is the wholehearted presence we can bring to ourselves when we're suffering and when we've fallen short of our ideals. It is the single most important tool for sustainable positive change in ourselves and the world.

Being kind to ourselves is challenging, as many of us tend to be our worst critics. We give much more grace, compassion, and understanding to a dear friend than we do ourselves. When a close friend tells us, "I messed up, I'm such a failure," we tell that person, "You are not a failure. This mistake does not define you as a human being. What you're going through is hard right now, but you are a good person and will get through this." However, when we experience those same feelings of failure and inadequacy, we are not as kind and accepting of ourselves. Even though we intellectually understand that no one is perfect and that we are flawed just like the rest of humanity, we expect near perfection from ourselves.

From a biological perspective, there are survival reasons for our tendency to hold ourselves to higher standards than others. Our early human ancestors had to fight for their needs such as food, water, and shelter. Appearing stronger and more capable was a useful method to getting our needs met. The dangers we faced then, generally speaking, were much more severe than they are in modern times. Defending our property and protecting our image were extremely important for our survival.

When we judge and criticize ourselves, we're attacking ourselves as if we are an enemy. We've been conditioned to have higher expectations of ourselves, but it no longer necessitates our survival. It can be scary to feel like we are not measuring up and like others don't perceive ourselves the way we desire. The key here is to stop beating ourselves up for our perceived failures, and when we catch ourselves beating ourselves up, stop beating ourselves up for beating ourselves up.

Being compassionate toward ourselves includes kindness toward ourselves when we realize we are being very unkind to ourselves. It's not helpful to tell ourselves, "I shouldn't feel this way." When we've made a mistake, or fallen short of our goal, our inner critic may show up and begin whispering harsh criticism in our ears,

"You're a failure. Why did you even try to attempt this? You're not good enough." Once we recognize what is happening internally and acknowledge the presence of our inner critic, we can say to them, "Hello, thank you for coming, I know you came to protect me, but I'm okay."

We can place our hands on our hearts and, as if we are talking to a friend or a child, say to ourselves, "I see you are hurting. I'm sorry you are suffering. It's okay to feel frustrated, angry, and disappointed. This is very difficult, and you are not a failure. You did not do as well as you had hoped, but that does not make you any less worthy of love and belonging. This struggle does not define you as a person. I'm here for you."

Once the inner critic has quieted, we can reflect on our suffering in the context of our shared humanity. We recognize that we are not unique in our suffering, that everyone else in the world is suffering in some way too, and that many others are experiencing the same suffering as we are at this very moment. We suffer just as everyone else in the world suffers, and we can expand our hearts to hold it all mindfully.

For many people, the ability to exercise compassion for themselves is extremely difficult and can feel unnatural or perhaps dangerous. If offering yourself kindness is too difficult, you can metaphorically call on another figure in your life who you know holds you with compassion. It may be a child, a friend, a partner, a parent or other family member, a pet, a spiritual figure, or your most awakened self. You can tap into the love, acceptance, and understanding that they offer you anytime you need it. When you recognize a difficult emotion arising, you can close your eyes and imagine this figure standing with you, perhaps embracing you or touching your shoulder, looking at you lovingly and offering kind words or just their gentle presence alone. Allow yourself to be fully immersed in the experience, bathing yourself in tenderness, understanding, and love.

The more we practice self-compassion, the more naturally it will come to us. We can offer ourselves kindness in times of difficulty, then release the pain instead of letting it weigh us down. Whereas shame and judgment trap us in a perpetual cycle of painful patterns, self-compassion frees us of the added weight by breaking the chains that bind us, allowing us to move forward more easily. The liberation we experience when we discover our ability to heal our own wounds and let go of shame and judgment is profound.

An important part of the practice of self-compassion requires that we turn toward our suffering, instead of instinctively turning away from it. Many of us have learned that certain emotions are "good" and others are "bad." Most people associate "bad" emotions with ones such as anger, frustration, abandonment, disappointment, rejection, insecure, and fearful. Because we have labeled these emotions as "bad," we deny their existence and refuse to acknowledge their presence. By swallowing our "bad" emotions and refusing to look at them, we become unfortunate victims to their disastrous resurfacing. When we are open and allow ourselves to be present with these difficult emotions mindfully, we gain insight into our suffering and allow space for healing and growth. The key to our deepest spiritual awakening lies in our ability to befriend these uncomfortable emotions.

Kintsugi is an ancient Japanese art form of repairing broken pottery with lacquer mixed with powdered gold. Instead of throwing away the broken pieces or trying to disguise them, the cracks are illuminated. The focal point of these art pieces become the broken edges, the imperfections. The beauty in our cracks and imperfections also depends on our careful, tender nurturing of these wounds.

It's important to recognize that any and all emotions are allowed and should be treated with tenderness and love. When difficult emotions arise, we can envision ourselves sitting at a long picnic table, much like the ones we may have eaten at in elementary school. We can picture our emotions as children, all wanting to sit with us at the table. During this practice, we are in charge of who's allowed to sit at the table, and our work is to allow anyone who wants to join to do so. No emotions get turned away.

Maybe Anger storms in, with their arms crossed across their chests and their noses and foreheads scrunched. We can gently smile at Anger and ask them if they'd like a seat at the table. We don't need to begin a discussion with Anger or ask them why they are the way they are. We just need to share space with them, and not turn them away. We can thank Anger for coming and tell them they can stay as long as they need. We can just sit in silence with Anger and breathe. Perhaps Shame comes in next, their clothes dirty and tattered. Shame might be reluctant to approach the table, for fear of being rejected. With the same kindness and acceptance as with Anger, graciously invite Shame to come sit with you and Anger at the table. Feelings of sadness or guilt, anger or frustration, even judgment and blame, all are allowed to come to the table of self-compassion.

All feelings are welcome.

All.

Instead of shutting ourselves down or shoving difficult emotions away, we need to stay open. We need to stay open with a mindful, tender, and loving awareness of our entire life experience. This is how we cultivate self-compassion and how we find inner strength to keep moving forward.

****

Awareness Exercise:

1. Begin practicing loving kindness meditations.

   A loving kindness, or metta meditation, is a practice for helping us see the goodness in ourselves and others. It allows us to break free from the "us versus them" mentality, recognizing our common humanity with everyone.

Many people struggle to extend loving kindness to themselves, so we will begin by imagining someone we love offering love to us, then we will move out from there. I will offer specific loving kindness phrases, but you can change them to whatever feels most authentic to you.

This kind of meditation may at times feel mechanical or awkward, and irritation or anger may arise. If this happens, extend patience and kindness to yourself for whatever arises.

Guided Loving Kindness Meditation:

Begin by finding a comfortable seated position and a posture that is upright and alert, yet comfortable.

Allow the eyes to gently close, or rest half open in a slight downward gaze. Begin with a quick scan of the body from head to toe, releasing any obvious tension. Unclench the jaw, allow the shoulders to ease down away from the ears, and relax the belly.

You may consider taking a couple of deep cleansing breaths and then allow the breath to be natural. Invite the breath to be your connection to the present moment.

Now visualize a wide-open sky—vast, blue, and expansive.

Imagine that you can see an impression of a smile in the sky. Sense into the openness and receptivity that this generates.

Now merge your mind with the sky, allowing the impression of the smile to spread down into your eyes. Let the corners of your eyes lift and your brow to soften. Then allow the smile to spread down to your lips in a slight smile.

Then invite the smile to spread down into your heart space and feel the expansion in your chest. Allow the shoulders to rest comfortably and the hands to become soft.
Sense into the space and openness that this creates and the gentle and kind presence that has come forward.

Now picture someone in your life who you love a lot, where the love comes easily and is uncomplicated. It could be a parent, a partner, a child, a pet, a spiritual figure. Take some time to reflect on the qualities that you most cherish about them. Maybe it's their humor, their kindness, their vitality for life.

Breathe gently and recite the phrases inwardly directed at them:

May you be safe and peaceful.
May you be healthy and happy.
May you know a deep and natural peace.
May you accept yourself just as you are.

Hold them in loving kindness in your mind, as you gently repeat these phrases.

Now imagine them lovingly gazing back at you, wishing for you too to be held in loving kindness.

Picture them saying to you kindly:

May you be safe and peaceful.
May you be healthy and happy.
May you know a deep and natural peace.
May you accept yourself just as you are.

Receive these wishes gracefully and allow them to repeat these well wishes to you. Note to yourself how it feels to receive this love.

Now take in the love and turn it toward yourself. You may consider placing a hand on your heart and saying to yourself:

May I be safe and peaceful.
May I be healthy and happy.
May I know a deep and natural peace.
May I accept myself just as I am.

Now picture a neutral person in your life that you're somewhat familiar with but for whom you don't have any strong negative or positive feelings.

Direct these well wishes to them:

May you be safe and peaceful.
May you be healthy and happy.
May you know a deep and natural peace.
May you accept yourself just as you are.

Now picture someone in your life with whom you have a difficult relationship—someone who evokes anger, fear, or hurt. Begin by taking a moment to try to see past the mask and to see some aspect of their basic goodness. It may even help to imagine them as a child or at the end of their life. Can you recall to yourself one quality about this person that you admire?

Remind yourself that all beings wish to be happy and avoid suffering and that life matters to this person just as it does to you.

When you're ready, recite the phrases inwardly directed to them:

May you be safe and peaceful.
May you be healthy and happy.

May you know a deep and natural peace.
May you accept yourself just as you are.

Repeat the phrases as you're able to do.

Take a moment to honor and reflect on the goodness that you've brought to this meditation—to a dear one, yourself, a neutral one, and a difficult one. Sense into your shared humanity, vulnerability, and basic goodness.

Now imagine that this loving presence that you've cultivated over the past few minutes is expanding and extending all around you, above and below you, all around you.

Recite the phrases internally to all living beings:

May all beings be safe and peaceful.
May all beings be healthy and happy.
May all beings know a deep and natural peace.
May all beings accept themselves as they are.

Take a moment to reflect on the loving presence that is here now. Dwell in this space of love and acceptance. This presence is more the truth of who you are than any other story you tell yourself. This is your true identity.

2. Start a RAIN meditation practice.

The RAIN meditation I learned was first created by Michele McDonald and later modified by Tara Brach. It is designed to help us grow our self-compassion when we are feeling overwhelmed by limiting beliefs. It is a useful tool we can bring to our practice in areas of our lives where we are feeling stuck, where we are feeling caught in our difficult emotions and tangled in the stories we've created.

Guided RAIN Meditation:

RAIN is an acronym. "R" stands for *recognize*, "A" for *allow*, "I" for *investigate*, and "N" for *nurture*. We will further explore these steps as we go through the meditation.

Begin by finding a comfortable position. It can be on a chair or on a bench or a cushion on the ground. Find a posture that is upright and alert, yet comfortable.

Allow your eyes to gently close and do a quick scan of your body from head to toe, releasing any obvious tension. Smooth the brow line, unclench the jaw, ease the shoulders down away from your ears, relax the belly.

Now begin by establishing presence in the moment by taking a couple of deep breaths and then allow your breath to be natural.

Bring your attention to wherever you most easily notice the breath or wherever it is experienced most pleasantly. It may be a cool tingling sensation in the back of your throat on the inhale, the rise and fall of your chest or belly, or the heat on your upper lip as you exhale.

Once you feel your mind settle a bit, bring to your mind a part of your life where you are feeling stuck, emotionally or mentally. It may be a conflict with a family member, a difficulty at work, a feeling of failure or inadequacy. Pick a situation that feels triggering, but not one that triggers past trauma.

Imagine the triggering scenario in as much detail as possible. Picture the room that you're in and the other people that may be present. Play the scene out in your head like a movie. Imagine the words that are said and the things that happen and then pause the "movie" right when you get to the part where you feel triggered.

Let yourself experience whatever feelings and emotions that arise. There might be sadness, fear, shame, anger, hurt, frustration.

Now we will begin with the "R" of RAIN: Recognize.

Pay attention to what is happening inside of you as you focus on this triggering moment. Gently whisper to yourself internally the physical sensations that are arising, the emotions that are present.

Now we move to the "A" of RAIN: Allow.

Ask yourself, "Can I be with this?"

Our tendency is to push away difficult emotions—to turn them away, to deny them, to ignore them. But instead, can you stay open to this emotion, to this experience? How can you make space for this? Allow yourself to be present with the sensations and emotions.

Now, move on to the "I" of RAIN: Investigate.

This is not a cerebral type of investigation, but more of a somatic experience. How is this experience manifesting in the body? Do you notice an aching? A tightness? A squeezing anywhere in your body? With curiosity and kindness, can you ask yourself, "What's the most difficult part of this experience? What am I believing?"

Maybe some beliefs that are coming up for you are: "I'm not good enough," "I'm not lovable," "I'm unworthy of love and belonging," "I'm a failure," "I'm not considered."

Allow yourself to assume the facial expression and the body posture that best suits whatever is coming up for you.

Where do you feel this most in your body?

If this vulnerable place could communicate, what would it want you to know?

Now move on to the "N" of RAIN: Nurture.

Ask yourself, "What does this vulnerable place most need from me? Are there any compassionate words I can offer or just a kind presence of acceptance and understanding?"

Bring to your mind a compassionate being who you would like to provide you comfort. It can be an image of a loved one, a parent, a child, a spiritual figure. It can even be an image of your future, most awakened self. Adjust your posture into this compassionate being and allow them to comfort you. Consider bringing your hand to your heart, letting the kind energy flow through your body. Offer yourself comfort from this kind and loving presence. You might consider saying to yourself, "You are loved. You are worthy. I see your pain, and I'm here with you. You are not alone."

Bathe in this sunlight of self-compassion. Let your body fill up with this healing and nurturing presence.

Now we move on to "after the rain."

Allow yourself to become aware of the quality of presence that's here now. How has it changed from the beginning of this meditation?

Allow yourself to rest in this space for a few more moments before opening your eyes.

Journal Exercises:

1. Imagine that a dear friend of yours has confided in you a mistake they made that they feel bad about. Imagine that they tell you they feel like they are a terrible person, that they are unworthy of love and belonging.
What might you say to this friend to help them?

2. Now reflect on a recent time that you made a mistake and reflect on the self-talk that happened afterward. Were you able to extend compassion, or was there more judgment?

3. What is standing between you and your ability to extend love and kindness to yourself, if anything at all?

Chapter 6: Open Awareness

Some changes look negative on the surface, but you will soon realize that space is being created in your life for something new to emerge.

—Eckhart Tolle

Clouds roll in overhead, and a gust of wind blows through. A gentle breeze brushes my cheek, as light and shadow dance in the aspen leaves. My bottom is firmly planted on the earth, and a dull, tingling sensation rises up my left leg. I resist the urge to immediately shift position. Birds converse overhead, and the clouds retreat, presenting the sun again. My body relaxes and opens to the change in temperature. I mindfully shift positions and notice the tingling sensation disappear.

Shadows. Coolness. Tingling. Swaying. Fluttering. Pressure. Throbbing. Judgment. Chirping. Light. Warmth. Relief. Gratitude.

Sensations, images, and sound elegantly glide in a harmonious dance of a well-constructed piece of art. Heat radiates from the sun, cascading over my shoulders. A bird glides through my field of vision, its image not to be clung to. Sounds and sensations arise and fall all around. Grounded to the earth, absorbed by the sun, I dissolve into awareness. Sitting in the midst of it all, I notice the separate "I" fading. My mind is like the sky, vast and expansive.

With nothing to do and nowhere to go, I rest in my true nature—my unstoried, unlabeled, unidentified self. I am not just me, but everything and everyone. I am vast, expansive, ever changing, and interconnected. I am the sun, the sky, the rock beneath me, and everyone around me. In this space, time is not a constraint, and possibilities are endless. The boundaries of who and how I am are challenged, as I see the true impermanent and interdependent nature of my existence. I am like this, and I am also not. Who am I? Is that really who I am? What am I?

A bell rings out, gently signaling the end of our open awareness meditation. Bowing to the sky, I express my gratitude to the earth for its living dharma, its teachings. I stretch my arms and shift positions, and I look around at the friendly faces here with me. Mark Coleman, insight meditation teacher and our retreat leader, invites us all to close our meditation.

I stretch out my legs and reach out my arms toward the sky, movement returning to my limbs. I wonder if the trees think we're strange because of our restlessness. One moment, we're planted and peaceful, the next we're fidgety and on the move. Do the trees know something about joy that we don't know?

We line up on the trail and mindfully walk through the thick brush, heading back to the lodge for dinner. Although no one is speaking, my ears receive a cacophony of sound—the crunch of dirt beneath our shoes, the swishing sound of our bodies rubbing against our hiking gear, the distant buzzing sound of some mysterious bug, and the leaves on the branches of the trees swaying in the wind, as if to say, "Come back soon."

As a student of Western education, a meditation retreat as a prerequisite to an educational program feels foreign to me. But here I am on a seven-day silent meditation retreat, with no cell phone service and no contact with my family. Preparing for this trip was difficult.

How could I possibly leave my children for a whole week with no contact? What kind of mother am I?

As I painstakingly weighed the option of coming or not, self-judgment arose fiercely. I didn't know any other mothers who had left their young children for an entire week, with no contact at all.

What if they think I don't care about them or miss them at all? Is my absence going to damage my relationship with my children?

Then I reflected on all the positive ways that Buddhism and mindfulness had impacted my life. I reflected on my darkest days, in the beginning of the pandemic, when I doubted my worthiness of life and love—the endless tears, the feelings of despair, loneliness and shame. Then I recalled how those stroller walks with my children and Noah's interpretation of the dharma saved my life. Mindfulness pulled me out of a deep, dark pit. I'm learning to stop shaming myself—to stop expecting perfection from myself. I'm experiencing the peace that arises from loosening my grip on labels. I'm learning to forgive those who have hurt me, to see how the pain they caused me was a result of their own internal suffering as well. Hurt people hurt people, and the people who hurt me were hurt a lot. I see their goodness now; I see beyond their hurtful actions. They've caused me suffering because they suffer so much. I am connected to them, and my healing is their healing. After years of therapy, antidepressants, healthy eating, and exercise, mindfulness has been the most powerful tool for me.

I want to bring this practice to others, to let it heal them like it has healed me. Being a mindfulness and meditation teacher will deepen my practice as well, making me a better version of myself. Self-care is not selfish.

I ultimately decided to go and hugged my family goodbye, hugging my children just a little longer before reluctantly pulling out of the driveway and heading on my way.

Subtle crying and sniffling sounds follow us as we hike back to the lodge. It's interesting to see how this retreat is unfolding for each person. Some people seem content, like this retreat is refreshing for them, while others seem like they're in pain. I notice my instinct to want to turn toward the owner of the tears and console them, but we each have made a vow of silence for the duration of the retreat. As unnatural as this feels to me, I imagine that perhaps this person feels held by the unity of silence in this community—a safe space to really *feel* the true depths of your emotions without the typical, everyday life pressures and expectations. I feel sad for her though and imagine my wish for her well-being is somehow helping her.

I collapse face-first on my bed and feel the rise and fall of my body with each breath. I take note of a subtle soreness in my back; I've never sat in meditation this long before. My brain is grateful, but my body is not. I think back to Alex and the kids at home. While I do miss them, I'm pleasantly surprised at how well I'm handling the separation. I'm actually enjoying my time here, more than I expected. I've never had an opportunity like this to take a deep dive into my practice. It's a novel experience for me to meditate for so long, without hearing shouts for my assistance with a snack or a small child crawling into my lap.

Tiny moments of guilt creep in, the old familiar critical voice telling me I'm a bad mother for doing this. But somehow, the voice feels softer, further away, and less believable. It doesn't suck me into its grip of shame. I quickly overcome each judgmental thought.

The dinner bell rings, jolting my sleeping body to alertness once again. I peel myself off my bed and head to the bathroom to wash up before dinner.

Dinner is absolutely delicious, as are all of our meals. I've never paid this much attention to a meal before. I've been practicing mindful eating on this retreat, paying attention to all my senses with each bite I take, focusing my attention on the sights, smells, and tastes, instead of letting myself get lost in thought. Meal time is commonly a social time, a time to reconnect with people around you. The vow of silence, however, means silent meals as well. At first I thought it would be strange, awkward even, but I'm finding it quite peaceful and relieving. I'm absorbed into the experience of eating as the vibrant colors and dynamic flavor provide a feast for my eyes and my tongue. I notice the moment I feel satiated, clean my dish, grab a cushion, and head to the porch for the evening meditation.

The early evening sun rests over the mountains, still radiating its light and warmth over the west-facing deck. I smile at the sun and set my cushion in a strip of its warm glow. I find myself in a comfortable seated position; relax the tension in my jaw, my brow line, and my shoulders, and center my attention on my breath. I relax back and open my awareness to the ever-changing world around me. Sounds arise and fall—the river splashing on the banks of the river below, birds chirping, leaves rustling. I notice thoughts arise and pass by, like clouds in an open sky. I notice my contact with the cushion, the heat on my skin, the breeze on my cheek, gentle vibrations throughout my body. My mind is expansive like the sky, open to the constant change of sensations, and I become unaware of where my body ends and the rest of the world begins. The harder I look for "me," the more difficult it is to find. Then all at once I dissolve into awareness itself, no longer the observer.

Today I returned to the sun.
The fire in my body, fueled
By the air it breathed,

Burst into flames,
And we were again one.

No resistance, I am unobstructed, expansive, and receptive to all that is here. Liberated from the ties I bind myself with, I discover a space where everything is welcome. Nothing is off-limits, nothing is too dangerous to look at. I am a vessel of open receptivity.

Out of nowhere, I am suddenly and unexpectedly crushed by a heaviness in my chest. The sensation of drowning takes over and my breath quickens beneath the mourning pressure. Unaware of why this is happening, I feel uneasy but try to stay present with it. Curiosity encourages my acceptance of these sensations, so I stay open without pushing it away or judging it. I feel small, blocked, and contracted. A tear rolls down my face, and my body trembles. *Hello, Loneliness. Hello, Sadness.*

I feel so lonely in my marriage, and I have felt this way for the past couple of years. The pandemic robbed me of my feelings of safety and robbed my spouse's attention. Loneliness inhabits our house and my soul, fueling my fear of abandonment. I see that Alex is finally making positive changes, yet I still feel overwhelmed by loneliness and sadness. Once a united front, an unbreakable team, we're now two lonely ships trying to navigate in the same direction, separately. The deep and compassionate love we once shared feels hollow and empty now.

Am I still in love with him? Should we still be together? What if it's too late for us?

I miss desire. I miss feeling desired. When I look at him now, I think of how he's hurt me. I feel angry, critical, and hurt. He doesn't feel like that soft place for me to land anymore, like he used to. He feels like someone who might hurt me again. He feels like someone who doesn't want me anymore like he used to.

Who can blame him? I've pushed him out of my heart.

The suffering I experienced as a result of his emotional abandonment has led to feelings of resentment. Anger and sadness still linger in my bones. Consumed by my own wounds, I've blocked my ability to recognize his suffering. I have made him an unreal other, capable of causing me pain, but unable to experience suffering himself. I know the truth, though, that he suffers too. Behind his sometimes empty eyes and vacant stare is a scared, hurting person. He feels scared, lonely, powerless, regretful, and sad. My falsely constructed two-dimensional image of his existence is shattered, as he becomes alive to me again. He is real, and I remember his realness in this moment. I feel as though I have just woken up from a long dream.

Suddenly, I am able to recognize and hold both of our suffering with deep compassion. When I suffer I explode, and when he suffers he shuts down. I can finally see clearly that his disengagement is not about me; it is just his default way of coping with difficult emotions. This is the expression of his pain. What I once recognized intellectually, I now know experientially. His coping with it by checking out, however, is a trigger for me. It rips open old wounds that have cut so deep into my soul.

I've been disconnected from my heart, unable to practice deep listening and compassion for him. I can see it all now, as painful as it is to acknowledge, how I too have caused him suffering. Filled with despair from the tragedies he witnessed, he comes home to a wife who criticizes his choices and momentary lapses of attention. He married my childhood trauma when he married me, and he has walked through dark times with me to get to where we are now.

Hello, Guilt.

Guilt rides in like an angry bull, crushing my throat. I have been trying to change him, to fit him into a mold of who I think he should be. I have been making him feel like he's not good enough. I have been feeling frustrated by him when he is suffering, causing him to suffer more by acting out my frustration in hurtful ways. He's not the only one who's done the hurting here.

An old, familiar voice arises, threatening to ruin me like it has tried to before.

I'm a bad wife.

I recognize this critical voice. I know I don't have to believe this thought, just as I don't have to believe I'm a bad mother, but I feel myself getting sucked into the shame.

He has apologized for staying away so long during the beginning of the pandemic, that he sees now that it was a mistake. He confided in me how scared and confused he was. I've had the intention to forgive him, but I'm not quite there yet.

Hello, Fear.

Fear creeps in, whispering, "I told you that you weren't good enough. He probably wants to leave you." Panic grabs my throat, choking me. I worry that with all the trauma I've experienced in my life, I have inadvertently hurt my husband, and now I may lose him. The damage I have done may be irreparable. I worry that maybe I've ruined our relationship and that even though he won't admit the plant is dead he knows deep down he doesn't want me anymore. I worry that we'll never again be whole, that I may have destroyed us.

Our entire relationship flashes before my eyes—our first date at a restaurant in Washington, DC, when I was the first to make a move by grabbing his hand (which he adamantly disagrees, claiming he made the first move). I think about the experiences we've had, the places we've traveled, the love and laughter and adventure we've shared. I think about our wedding day. I think about the tears in his eyes as I walked down the aisle toward him. I think about when he first became a father, the love in his eyes when he looked at his son.

He was immediately the best father I'd ever known. I think about how he carried so much of our pain with our son's health problems, how he comforted me when I was scared. I think about how he comforted me when I lost that second pregnancy. I think about how much love and support he's given me when I've lost family members and how he's always seen the best in me, even when I can't. I think about him becoming a father to our baby girl, watching how his heart expanded for her.

Then I wonder if he still would look at me the same way if I were to walk down that aisle today. Would there be tears of love in his eyes or resentment? Would *I* still feel the same? He's always seen the best in me, made me feel like a better person when I doubted my self-worth. I can't honestly say I've always held him with the same level of compassion. This realization is crushing me, drowning me, and I desperately want him to know how good a husband, father, and friend he is.

I want to run away, to hide in my room, to pack up my things and head back home. These emotions feel dangerous, and my instinct screams, "Shut down! Shut it all down!" But I tell myself I can stay, at least for another hour.

Whenever my children have a nightmare about a monster, I tell them to look at the monster in the face. When they look at it, I say, it won't be so scary anymore, and the monster will lose its power and go away. Monsters feed off the fuel of our fear, so dig down deep in the bravest part of yourself and stand tall and turn around to face it.

I thought I had faced all my monsters. Dismantling the belief of being a "bad mother" has been a monumental task, and I feel frustrated that there's yet another monster I have to face.

Can I hold myself with compassion when the belief of "I'm a bad wife" arises, just as I've held myself with compassion before?

I'm in distress, struggling to find the ability to find comfort in my practice. I force myself to sit like a Buddha statue, tall and still, with the exception of the moments when I am trying to catch my breath. I feel like ants are crawling all over me, and the wind is trying to suck the air out of my body. The bell rings, announcing the end of the meditation. I fumble with my mat and attempt to leave as quickly, and discreetly, as possible.

I've lost the ability to feel held by this community of kind people, and I suddenly feel disconnected from these strangers. I need to be alone, to decompress without being surrounded by everyone.

I head upstairs to my private room, grab my towel, and dash to the shower. I feel the mounting pressure in my chest. I rip off my clothes and enter the shower just as the dam explodes. I lean on the wall to support my weight as everything comes bursting out. Tears and snot roll down my face, washing down the drain with the water. I attempt to muffle my cries, not wanting any attention from anyone. My chest hurts and my tears don't stop, my body struggling to maintain the strength to stand. I carefully lower myself to the shower floor, feeling the beating of the water on my back as I desperately seek relief from the pain.

All of me wants to shut this down, to tell myself to think of something else, to distract myself, but I don't know how. This feels too big to put away. I need to find balance in the midst of this wave of emotion, but it feels like a tsunami.

Should I leave my husband? Does he deserve better than me? Can we find each other again and share the same love we used to?

No answers show up for me. No reassurance comes. But eventually, the tears stop, and I stare at the wall as I sit curled up on the shower floor. I know I have been in here long enough and need to get out, even though it's uncomfortable.

I wrap my towel around me and walk back to my room. Looking down at my feet, I carefully put one foot in front of the other.

I don't think I can stay. I need to go home, to tell Alex what I've realized. To tell him I don't know what I need. To ask him if there's still love here. To ask him if he can forgive me and still really loves me.

I sit on my bed and contemplate leaving the retreat. If I leave now, I will not fulfill my prerequisite for the mindfulness meditation teacher certification course. I will have to do this again, and I'm already halfway through. So much coordination has gone into allowing me to be here, with Alex and his mom taking time off work so someone will always be with the kids. If I stay, maybe I'll get some clarity on this. If I'm being honest with myself though, so much of me wants to ignore this, to bury it deep down inside me. I keep reminding myself that running away from this monster will not make it go away, but it's painfully difficult to stay with it. I want to stay, to finish this, but I feel terrified and want to run home to my husband.

I have so much guilt for the thoughts and feelings I'm having. I instinctively want to run home to my husband, to seek comfort from him. It doesn't seem fair though for him to comfort me when I'm feeling guilty for how I've treated him and for having second thoughts about our marriage. But he's who I've always turned to when I'm in pain, so I am extremely conflicted.

Since I've had this realization, it's been a little over an hour and a half. I've finished my meditation and showered. Maybe now I can do the next thing. Step by step.

I put my clothes on, then look at my watch. The evening dharma talk begins in twelve minutes. I check my face in the mirror, hoping there's not too much puffy evidence of my crying, and then head back downstairs to make a cup of chamomile tea. I can't promise myself I'll make it through the rest of the retreat, four whole more days, but I can make it through the next dharma talk.

I struggle but try to focus my attention on the teachings—to bring my awareness to the warmth of the mug in my hands, the earthy flavor of the tea as I sip it. I think about my hurting marriage.

Yes, there is pain... and there is nice warm tea.

I am okay again for a moment, finding some contentment in the comfort of tea. Then the fear of what to do and what all this means returns.

What if we're not meant to be together anymore? Can we find love again? Can we ever truly trust each other again? Do I still deserve him?

Noticing that my thoughts are spiraling and waves of panic are starting to roll in again, I bring my attention to the sensation of my feet on the floor and take a few slow deep breaths.

Yes, there is fear... and there is this wonderful dharma talk.

I continue to pendulate between the pain and the things that are nourishing me. The dharma talk finishes, and I head upstairs to bed.

It's been three hours since I had this revelation. I'm still here, still breathing, still safe. Can I make it through the night?

I lay my head on my pillow and try to will myself to sleep. I suspect that if I go home now, if I instinctively run home to my husband and have him console me, I won't be able to look deeply into these emotions.

The most compassionate thing I can do for my marriage is to stay here and see what I uncover.

Sleep eventually comes, and I wake up to my alarm, notifying me that it's time to get up and help with breakfast prep. Each of the students has a yogi duty, and mine is breakfast prep. I enjoy chopping the veggies while gazing out of the window at the sunrise.

The last four days of the retreat drag on. I bring the intention to stay with the pain and, when it becomes too intense, to ask myself what else is present. "Yes, and …" is the name of the new game I play to pull myself out of the whirlpool when I start to feel like I'm drowning. Every single day, I struggle multiple times with the desire to run home. And every day, I remind myself of my intention—to stay open to my emotions and experience and to live my most authentic life. After all, how can I teach mindfulness to others if I can't practice it, even in difficult times? As excruciating as it is, I stay.

Though the waves of panic, fear, and guilt continue to cycle, the intensity of them lessens over time. I also discover more spaciousness and more moments of clarity. I spend a lot of my alone time crying and writing in my journal. I resolve to spend the rest of my retreat staying open to the pain when I can tolerate it and to be honest with myself about what I want.

I spend time imagining a life without Alex. I imagine finding someone else, who is perhaps also vegan and practices Buddhism. I sincerely let myself experience the thought of this option. I think about who Alex and I were when we first met and how much we've changed. The nature of impermanence can be both extremely comforting and absolutely terrifying. I imagine this supposed alternative partner of mine being the "perfect" fit for who I am in this moment; then I imagine us both changing over time, as nature dictates. I imagine this person hurting me in some way, which inevitably happens in all relationships.

I reflect on how I've been hurt by Alex and all the ways he's helped me. I notice that what feels more prevalent to me at this moment are all the ways he has made my life better. The memories and important moments that come flooding to me in these moments are all the ways he's shown up for me in our relationship, all the ways he's loved me exactly the way I want to be loved.

As the days in retreat go on, the more I honestly realize that Alex is still who I want to be with. My heart starts to break open; all the walls I've put up to him come crashing down, and I discover that my heart is still inextricably tied to his. The thought of losing him is unbearable. He is my partner, and he is perfect for me. He is exactly who I want to spend my life with.

There is some relief in this discovery, and yet I still have fear—fear that I've hurt him too much to fully accept me back into his heart. I know the pain of feeling like I'm not good enough, and knowing that I've caused him the same pain crushes me. I decide to write him a letter. I feel clear-headed and know what I want to say and what I want to ask.

I struggle to write the letter through watery eyes. I write to him about my revelation, the fear and guilt that consumed me during my meditation one evening. I write about how I noticed I've blocked him out of my heart and how sorry I am for how I've hurt him. I acknowledge how I've tried to change him and recognize how painful that must have been, and I tell him how he is perfect just the way he is. I write to him that more than anything, I want to work on our relationship and to nurture our love again. I end by asking him if he can forgive me and if he still wants to be in this marriage.

Can I trust him to tell me his honest truth? Will he admit it if the plant is dead?

I want to know his truth, even if it crushes me. If I have hurt him too much and he wants to move on, I need to know. I love him, and he deserves happiness.

I pack up my bag on the final morning of retreat and head home after breakfast. I consider calling Alex on my way home, but ultimately, I decide that what will serve me best is silence on our way home.

On our final retreat evening, Mark Coleman challenged us to make one commitment to ourselves, some way of honoring what we'd learned from being here. I made two vows to myself. One was a vow to bring more silence into my life— to sometimes shut off the podcast while I'm driving and to put my phone away and look around me when I walk outside after getting off work. I discovered at the retreat how healing silence can be and how inclined I usually am to fill up the space with distractions. My final and most important vow was to practice compassion for Alex.

Compassion for others starts with compassion for self. I've been practicing self-compassion for a long time, because that's what I needed. Now, I finally feel like I have the energy to practice it for others. I can see beyond my own pain and want to help reduce his pain.

Driving feels a bit over stimulating after processing things so slowly over the last week. All the cars and street lights I pass feel jarring, and I haven't even made it back to the city. I breathe deeply and sit in silence the whole way home, watching my experience as I reintegrate.

I pull into the driveway and put the car in park. Jack is in school still, so I know it's Alex and Everly waiting inside for me. I close my eyes and follow my inhale, a cool tingling sensation in the back of my throat and my belly expanding, and think to myself, "Calm." I exhale slowly, feeling the warmth of my breath on my upper lip, and think, "Ease."

Here goes nothing. I can be brave.

I walk into the house, and Everly runs to greet me.

"Mommy, Mommy, Mommy!"
I kneel down and embrace her, my hands tangled in her long blond hair, and a smile spreads across my face. I kiss her on her forehead.
"Evie, I missed you so much, baby girl! I'm so happy to see you!" I tell her.

I hold her for a minute longer, then stand up and look at Alex. I feel like I am looking at him in a way I haven't seen him in so long, like the day I walked down the aisle to him. I walk toward him and allow myself to be enveloped in his arms that are outstretched toward me. My body starts trembling, and tears begin rolling down my face. He rubs the back of my head and tenderly looks at me, a bit of worry in his eyes.

"Oh, honey, are you OK?" he asks.

I can clearly see his beauty again, his goodness that I had forgotten, that I had let get washed away in all the mess of life. I feel crushed as I think of all the ways I know I've made him feel like he wasn't good enough. I think of a quote by Wes Angelozzi, "Go and love someone exactly as they are. And then watch how quickly they transform into the greatest, truest version of themselves. When one feels seen and appreciated in their own essence, one is instantly empowered." I see and trust his goodness again. All my walls are down.

"Yes," I say through sobs, "I just missed you so much." I cry.

He pulls me closer and holds me tighter.

"I missed you too, honey," he says.

My heart feels raw and open, in a way it hadn't in years. I let him hold me for a while longer before I pull back to look at him and begin to explain a little, as much as I can in front of Everly.

"I didn't realize how much I'd miss you. I worried so much I'd struggle with how much I'd miss the kids, and I did miss them, but nothing was as painful," I pause to slow my breathing and tears, "as the realization of how much I miss *us*."

He looks a little shocked, like he wasn't expecting this from me. He immediately pulls me into his arms again and holds me.

"That sounds so hard, honey. I'm so sorry you had to go through that. I definitely want to hear more about what you mean by that," he consoles me.

I lean back and tell him I'd like that, and that I actually have a letter for him to read tonight after the kids are in bed. He kisses me on my lips, and I think to myself how happy that makes me feel and how I hope I am still the one he wants to be kissing.

That evening after the kids are in bed, I read him the letter, struggling to fight back my tears. I read each line, sitting cross-legged on the floor, occasionally glancing up at him on the couch. One escapes my grip and rolls down my cheek. I breathe deeply and continue reading until I've reached the end, when I ask him to please take time to contemplate whether or not there is still love to be had here and whether or not he still wants to be with me.

My eyes make contact with his, and a few more tears escape down my cheek.

"I'm sorry," I confess. "I don't want you to make a decision based on my crying. I want to know what you really want."

The last thing I want is for him to deny his own experience because he feels like he needs to protect me. I want him to feel safe to tell me how he really feels, even if that means telling me he's realized he doesn't love me the same way anymore.

"Heather," he began, "you have hurt me, that is true. Hearing how much you care about my pain feels good. I have hurt you too, so please don't feel alone in that."

I nod and stay quiet, breathing deeply to help me stay centered and calm.

"I know," he continues, "that you have struggled with the fear of us not working out. But that is never ever something I have thought about, honestly."

"But now I'm asking you," I urge him. "I'm asking you to think about it. I'm asking you to really consider whether or not you still want to be with me or if maybe I've done too much damage to you and you can't love me the same anymore. I'm asking if you'd possibly be happier leaving me for someone else. I really want you to take an honest look at your feelings and tell me when you know."

"Heather," he says, sincerely, "I already know. There is no one in the world that I want to be with more than you. You are loving. You are funny. You are passionate, and our whole family is better because you are in it. We have hurt each other, that is true, but I still love you. I still want to be with you."

"OK," I say.

The tears that I've been holding back come bursting forth, and I cover my face and buckle over. My body relaxes, in all the places I hadn't realized were tense, and relief washes over my body.

"Heather," Alex says gently, "are you sure you still want to be with me? I don't want to lie, it makes me feel worried that you seriously questioned our relationship."

I see the fear in his eyes, an emotion I know intimately. I can answer this question without hesitation. I crawl over to him, put my hands in his lap, and look into his eyes.

"Alex," I announce, "there is not a shred of doubt in my mind that you are exactly who I want to be with. I know it sounds scary what I experienced, and it was, but please believe me when I tell you that I had time. All I had was time. Time to consider who I am now, what I want, and if I still love you the same way. It was hard to go through, but I made myself stay open to it, so I would know for sure how I really feel. This is where I landed, back with you. You are exactly who I want, and I mean that with all my heart."

"Okay." He lets out an exhale. "I believe you."

He pulls me into his lap, and I kiss him through my salty tears. I look at him and tell him how much I love him and that I hope he knows how sorry I am for all the pain I've caused—that I have a plan to extend my compassion practice to him.

We hold each other for a longer time than I can remember us doing. Life has gotten so busy and so fast. There are so many little daily struggles—mending a skinned knee, calming an upset child, patiently waiting while a child struggles to put their shoes on, fixing broken toys while cooking dinner, bargaining with a child to sleep in their own bed. Seeing each other and truly connecting has become more difficult since we've become parents. But Alex's embrace feels the same as it always has. It feels safe, it feels warm, and it feels like home.

Eventually, we peel off each other. He brushes my hair behind my ear and kisses my forehead.

"You OK?" he checks.

"Yeah, I'm OK." I nod and smile. "You?"

"Yeah, I'm OK," he answers.

"Would you like to see something I've been working on?" he asks.

"Yes, please," I say, excited for a change in pace.

He holds my hand and guides me to the garage, where he shows me his latest project.

"I'm thinking about making coffee pour overs," he says, his eyes sparkling. "This is my first prototype."

Alex started his new job at the surgery center in May, and it is now the end of September. The first couple of months were tough on him. He struggled with guilt about leaving the ICU and with the feeling that he wasn't making as big of a difference in people's lives. The new job, however, is easier for him. He's very busy putting in IVs, prepping patients for surgery, helping them recover when they're done, and educating them, but the emotional toll is much less severe. Alex isn't dealing with death and grief on a weekly basis. When he comes home, he's tired but not distraught and disconnected from us.

I've slowly watched the light return to his eyes over the past few months. I've witnessed his reawakening to his life and the world around him. He's no longer constantly stuck in a mental limbo of the trauma he's seen. When he's home, he's actually home. When he eats, he eats. He's returned to his body and the unfolding experience of his life. I feel like I have someone back that I've missed for such a long time.

He has made a clearing in his mind, allowing for more playfulness and curiosity. He smiles more, laughs more, is more engaged in conversation, and plays with the kids. He's discovered a passion for woodworking, and he spends a lot of his down time in the garage creating things. He tells me he's interested in trying to sell the coffee pour overs, but if they don't sell, that's okay. He's enjoying himself anyway.

I'm not a woodworker. I don't know or care much about grain pattern or which saw does what. But I see what talking about woodworking does for Alex, so I love to listen to him tell me all about it. He lights up. His eyes sparkle. He's curious, contemplative, and creative.

"It's beautiful, Alex," I tell him. "I love it. I can't believe you made this; it looks so professional!"

"Really, you think?" he says, looking back down at the pour over.

He starts telling me all the techniques he has used to produce it and what changes he's thinking about making for the next one. His voice and project become the backdrop to the most beautiful work of art I've seen—my partner experiencing joy. My heart expands, and I feel more spacious in my body, heart, and mind.

Our awareness expands, and we hold it all—hurt from our relationship aches and pains, fear of not knowing what will become of us, courage to deepen our intention to love one another, gratitude for feeling seen and accepted, and joy of witnessing well-constructed art.

****

When we suffer, we contract, experiencing our small self instead of who we fully are. We have a natural resistance to pain, a tendency to pull back and shut down when we are hurt. But if we can find a way to relax and open, we will find more spaciousness around the pain. The pain is still there, but it is not all that is there.

Open awareness meditation is a practice we can use to find more spaciousness around our pain. Finding this relaxed and open awareness is possible anywhere, but it seems to come more readily when we're out in nature. Nature has a unique way of nurturing and healing us. Simply by resting in spacious awareness outdoors in nature, we can reconnect with our true nature, strip ourselves of all of our layers of identities, and just "be." Nature is the most nonjudgmental friend that we'll ever have. Nature will never judge us for how we're dressed, how successful we are in our careers, or for any of the choices we've made. It is always there, waiting for us to come be with it, and it accepts all of us and helps us see things as they truly are, without the storylines we create.

We can find a place in nature to sit, take a moment to arrive in the space, and reconnect with the elements inside and outside of our body. Oxygen is the most abundant element in the human body, present in almost every cell and necessary for our survival. So is this element present in our earth's crust, the air we breathe, and every water molecule that fills our oceans and other bodies of water. All human and other animal oxygen needs are supported by a process plants go through for their energy needs called photosynthesis. During photosynthesis, plants capture carbon dioxide and water, then use energy from the sun to transform it into energy for themselves and release oxygen back into the air. Carbon is the second most abundant element inside our bodies, functioning as building blocks to proteins, carbohydrates, and fats and providing us with energy. The earth's carbon is the foundation for all life and is stored in rocks, sediments, and the ocean. When humans and other animals exhale, we release carbon dioxide into the air, which can damage our atmosphere. But as stated before, the plants serve to protect our atmosphere by capturing the carbon dioxide we exhale. The calcium that strengthens our bones and assists in other functions of the body is also present in the earth's crust and other living organisms. The list goes on, including elements inside our bodies that are also present on the earth. What becomes clear is that although we tend to see ourselves as separate from the earth, we see that we are made up of the same basic elements. What also becomes clear is that we have a symbiotic relationship with the earth. We affect the earth, and the earth affects us. Our relationship with the earth is interdependent and interconnected.

Tapping into this energy of interdependence and oneness with the earth, we can rest in the spacious awareness this lends to. We sit in the elements and realize that we too are elements. We recognize our symbiotic relationship with nature and begin to feel a deep connection to our Mother Earth.

Once we feel like we have arrived into our true nature, our elemental beings, we can practice open awareness meditation. During open awareness meditation, we may practice with our eyes open, fixed on a spot in the far distance but open and aware of everything in our peripheral vision. One way to achieve this is to hold our arms out front with both index fingers pointing up in the center of our vision, then widen our arms as far as we can still hold our index fingers in our visual awareness. Our gentle gaze should be open and relaxed, including everything in our periphery.

We can then begin to anchor ourselves in the present moment by noticing what is present, with a gentle, relaxed attention. This attention to the present moment includes what is happening internally, as well as externally. We may take note of the sunlight on our skin and the warmth we feel, the sound and sensation of a gentle breeze, the vision of a bird taking flight and passing through our line of vision, and the scent of a nearby pine tree. We also take note of what is happening internally. We notice the breath, deep or shallow; the feeling of our buttocks on our cushion or bench; and any tension, tingling, and other sensations. We notice our tendency to cling to pleasant experiences, such as the sun's warmth, and our aversion to unpleasant experiences, such as a strong, cold wind that hits our face.

When we notice that we are lost in thought, we can invite a gracious and nonjudgmental recognition and tell ourselves, "Thinking," then gently bring our attention back to the present moment. We can practice this gentle noticing and naming each time we notice our attention has strayed from the present moment. We can say to ourselves, "Thinking," or "Judging," or "Planning," when we notice where our attention has gone. During open awareness meditation, we can choose to either use our breath or the vast space of awareness we are open to as our anchor.

It is very common for strong, unpleasant emotions to rise during meditation. We may feel overwhelmed by a strong sense of sadness, fear, or guilt. Our natural response may be to push it away, to shove it down and ignore it. These unpleasant experiences are gold though, when it comes to our own awakening to what is true. If instead of constantly shoving those experiences away, we stay open to them, we heal and learn about ourselves.

This practice should be exercised with caution with those who have a history of trauma. The more we learn to relax and open, we become more receptive to our experience, which may include resurfacing of old and unhealed wounds. In such a case where a meditator discovers deeply traumatizing memories and discomfort in their practice, it is wise to stop the practice and find a trauma informed therapist. With therapy and time, people who have a history of trauma often return to finding safety and expansion in their practice.

Even for those without a history of trauma, this can be an incredibly difficult practice, as it is very natural for us to want to immediately push away any strong, unpleasant emotions. These strong and unpleasant emotions, however, can be our greatest teachers. When an unpleasant emotion arises, we may feel a contraction inside ourselves. We may experience a metaphorical wall going up between ourselves and that strong emotion, a coping mechanism we have built to protect ourselves from pain. The problem with this contraction and this wall, however, is that it alienates us from the emotion we're experiencing and doesn't allow for acceptance or healing. The contracting, the turning away from these unpleasant experiences, leads to ignorance. It leads us to living a less authentic life, disconnected from the roots and truth of our existence.

When an unpleasant emotion arises, we should continue to maintain the same relaxed, open awareness we have been practicing.

We should notice the contracting with loving awareness and relax into it. We should notice what we feel in our bodies and relax in any areas with tension. We can invite the emotion to be with us as it needs, like a small child who is in distress and needing to be held and understood.

If the emotion becomes too difficult to stay with, we can re-open our awareness to what feels nourishing, such as our breath or the sun's warmth on our skin. Then, when we feel more stable, we can bring our attention back to the emotion. We can invite the unpleasant emotion back into our awareness and sit with it once we feel more stable again. This conscious attuning of our attention to what feels wholesome when we are experiencing much difficulty with an unpleasant emotion is known as "resourcing." Resourcing is a critical tool for us to utilize when we are open and allowing everything in, including the painful emotions.

I've playfully come to call this the game of "Yes, and…" In the game of "Yes, and…," we are fully open to all that is present; we invite both the pleasant and the painful emotions in, and when we notice an unpleasant emotion is becoming too overwhelming, we resource. For me, at the retreat with Mark Coleman, my game went a little like this: "Yes, there is a monstrous wave of guilt I am feeling, and there is the breeze through the aspen trees and the sun on my skin." At times, I spent a long time resourcing before I was able to return to the painful emotion. At one point, I almost left the retreat because of how strong my unpleasant emotions were. I knew that by leaving I was giving into the contracting and letting that wall I built between myself and my emotions remain up. I knew that if I stayed I would have to remain with my unpleasant emotions with no escape, and that felt terrifying to me. Intellectually, I understood I could benefit by staying. Experientially, I felt like I was suffocating, drowning in my strong, unpleasant emotions.

I chose to stay for the remainder of the retreat, and I'm so glad I did. I let myself feel the strong emotion of guilt and sadness. I felt the weight, the pressure in my chest, and stayed with the emotion as long as I could. Then when it became too much, I played "Yes, and…," and I brought my attention to what was nourishing. Being that the retreat was in the wilderness, it was not hard to find something beautiful, something nourishing to bring my awareness to. Being in nature is naturally healing. This process was not easy; it was actually one of the hardest things I have ever done, and I have done a lot of hard things in my life, including giving birth to two children. But when I left at the conclusion of the retreat, I had made peace with the emotion I was feeling. I could talk about it, acknowledge its existence, and though it was still difficult, it did not feel as crippling. I had a profound sense of clarity that came from staying with the emotion when my amygdala was screaming, "Danger! Run away!"

When we experience strong emotions that create discomfort and fear, it is as if we are being hijacked by our amygdalas. The fear center of our brain may process these strong emotions as a threat to our safety, so we instinctively begin to try and rid ourselves of this "dangerous" emotion. It's similar to having a nightmare about something trying to hurt us. In our dreams, we perceive ourselves as unsafe and in danger, and the emotional experience can be incredibly distressing, sometimes even for a few moments after we wake up, and we ground ourselves in reality when we realize we're not in any real danger. Some people have encountered lucid dreams, where they are aware they are dreaming while they are in the dream. Lucid dreamers can realize they are in a nightmare, face the monster instead of running away from it, and watch the monster dissolve as it loses its power.

Much like in a nightmare, we too can become hijacked by our fear and strong emotions while we are awake. The emotions can become so extreme that without our gentle awareness of what is happening inside our bodies we place ourselves in a state of reactivity. A reactive state of mind differs from a responsive state, in that when we are reactive our words and actions are driven by fear and anguish. When we go about our lives reacting to our environment instead of responding to it, we inevitably cause ourselves and others more suffering and we are not able to find inner peace. When we are responsive to these strong, negative emotions arising in our bodies, however, we burst open a tiny yet powerful space where we give ourselves agency by choosing how to tend to the strong emotions.

When reactivity takes over during the experience of an unpleasant emotion, we may also feel as if we need to shield ourselves from the experience in order to protect ourselves. This can look like "shutting down" when we're confronted with an unpleasant emotion, or quite literally running away from a retreat that is causing you to acknowledge painful truths that you've buried deep inside. Our heart contracts, unwilling to let our bodies feel the emotion, because it feels scary, unsafe.

As with lucid dreaming, if we are able to stop running from the monster, or the unpleasant experience, if we are able to stay with the uncomfortability, the emotion will eventually pass. Our work lies in our ability to rest with the uncomfortable emotions, to neither shove them down nor push them away. We may feel like we are going to lose control, but in reality, we give ourselves great agency by tending to uncomfortable emotions.

Just as changing weather patterns are a natural process of the earth's balance, changing emotions are a natural part of being human. Rainy days and sadness aren't "bad." Without the rain, there would be no plants, no oxygen created by those plants, and in turn no human and other animal life in existence. There is no good or bad weather; there is only weather.

This very notion is helpful to carry with us when tending to our internal weather. There are no good or bad emotions; there are only emotions. Fear and anger are not bad; they are just emotions. Like the rain, like the thunder and lightning, it will pass. If instead of contracting, we relax and open, the unpleasant experience will be able to flow in and out of us more easily.

Sometimes our biggest monsters are our best teachers. That is what makes the path of mindful awareness so unique to some other healing strategies. There is not one "cure," not one answer that will work for everyone, and we are our own best teachers. When something scares us and we want to contract, to shield ourselves from a storm, we should instead try to relax and open and learn.

We may prefer the sunny, storm-free days. Whatever weather we prefer, however, does not generate the weather we will experience. People have perfected the art of creating a space we call home, where we are protected from the elements we wish to shelter ourselves from, but weather is still happening, still changing at all times all around us.

We may grumble with frustration when it begins to rain if we had plans to go for a sunny hike, but we are comforted in knowing that the rain will pass. We also know, perhaps sometimes more intellectually than experientially, that rain is something to welcome because it is necessary to the earth's survival. Weather is just weather, neither good nor bad, yet we all tend to have an affinity for a certain type of weather. Whether or not we acknowledge and welcome our internal weather, it will continue to be there.

Fear, guilt, sadness, anger, and other unpleasant emotions can be great teachers to us. They can teach us a lot about ourselves and how our past experiences are shaping how we're interacting with and perceiving the events in our lives now. We may not always have the insight as to what is triggering such a strong emotion, but understanding the "why" is not necessary in order to be with emotion and let it pass.

When we are aware of what our triggers are, this can be very useful to us to be able to navigate our lives more skillfully. We will still likely experience the conditioned internal response that we have as a result of the stimulus, but having conscious awareness of what is happening to us in the moment can lessen the suffering it causes us and give us an opportunity to respond instead of react.

After a rainstorm passes and the clouds part, the sun will begin to shine once again and warm our bodies, the birds will begin chirping and flying overhead, the insects will crawl back out from their shelters and explore. We will feel the change in the external weather, and we will have a sense of our bodies' response to the storm's retreat and the sun's return. The change in weather can cultivate feelings such as gratitude, joy, or awe. We might notice physical sensations as well, such as a feeling of opening in our heart space, a gentle smile forming at the corners of our lips, a more relaxed, easy presence in our bodies.

We once again reflect on our elemental connection to the earth and feel nourished by the earth's gifts of sun and warmth, as well as rain and cool breezes. No matter how much we wish for the sun to always stay out and for the rainy, icy weather to stay away, the weather will continue to change. The only thing we truly have control over is our response to the changes.

No matter how much we meditate, no matter how dedicated we are at our practice, we will inevitably continue to experience the full range of emotions, just as we cannot control the external weather. All we can do is relax and be open to every experience. We can attune our attention to the gratitude and joy we feel when it arises, and we can relax and open to the grief and sadness when it emerges.

We are not separate from the earth; we are the earth. We are composed of non-human elements, put together into a specific combination and order that makes us human.

As a species, we tend to complicate the suffering that exists as a natural consequence of just being alive. We often create meaning where there may be no meaning. Perhaps we are interviewed for a job but are not selected for the position. All we know for sure is that we applied, we were interviewed, and we did not get chosen. The disappointment that we didn't get the job is the first layer of suffering that exists, which is out of our control. The problem, however, is that we don't usually stop there. We often add our own narrative and, worse, choose to believe it. If we tell ourselves, "I didn't get the job because I am not good enough, and I don't have enough experience," we create another layer of suffering for ourselves.

This notion is referred to as the second arrow of suffering in Buddhism. We don't have control over whether or not we will be hit with first arrows; they happen as a consequence of just being alive.

The first arrow in this situation is being denied a job you wanted. The second arrow, the suffering that we add to the situation, would in this case be the stories we create about why we didn't get the job, allowing it to cause us extra suffering.

Avoiding second arrows requires conscious effort. It relies on our ability to take a moment to step back, while in the middle of a storm, and ask ourselves what we're adding to the situation. It requires us to step out of our narrow view of our situation, in order to gain a wider view and consider things we hadn't noticed before. The more we practice stepping back and having curiosity about each situation in our lives from a broader perspective, the less we will suffer and the more we begin to realize we know a lot less about the reasons things happen to us than we presume to know.

We are biologically primed to focus our attention on things that induce fear and anger and other undesired emotions, and this lends to the perception of our lives to seem unsatisfactory. The more we practice open awareness meditation, either formally while in meditation or informally by creating moments of awareness of positive feelings and sensations throughout our day, we can cultivate more joy and gratitude in our lives.

Where there is suffering, there is also space for contentment. Throughout our lives, we may experience anger, frustration, jealousy, disgust, contempt, fear, sadness, aversion, guilt, and grief. We also have the opportunity to experience and cultivate joy, awe, contentment, happiness, gratitude, acceptance, delight, serenity, and hope. We can be an open vessel for the unwanted emotions to flow through, like a moving river. We can remain open and draw our attention to the nourishing things in our lives and let them fill us up.

Just like the earth, we are subject to change. We are elements that respond and react to the environment around us. We can begin to see our true nature, as a collection of elements and cells, and begin to experience the dichotomy between our true nature and the selves we present to the world.

Rejecting our worldly expression of self is not necessary in order to live our lives more authentically, but acknowledging that it is just an expression, an adaptation to navigate in our communities, can serve us to not feel so attached to those identities. Nature is always waiting for us to return, to allow us to reset and to remind us of our true nature.

****

Awareness Exercise:

1. Begin an open awareness meditation practice.

   An open awareness meditation is a practice that helps us cultivate equanimity, or the ability to find peace and composure in the midst of pleasure and pain, joy and sorrow, constant change—that is, the full human experience.

   Unlike in focused meditations, in an open awareness meditation, the attention is not focused on one anchor, such as the breath. Instead, we rest in choiceless awareness—a non-judgmental, receptive presence of our entire experience.

   We cultivate a mind that is open and vast like the entire sky, where thoughts, sensations, and emotions are like clouds, weather, and birds simply passing by.

   Buddhist monk Shunryu Suzuki says, "When we realize the everlasting truth of everything changes and find our composure in it, we find ourselves in Nirvana."

Guided Open Awareness Meditation:

Begin by finding a relaxed seated position, one that is comfortable and alert.

Scan the body and release any obvious tension. Smooth the brow line, loosen the jaw, relax the shoulders away from the ears, soften the belly.

Bring the attention to the breath, beginning with a few deep cleansing breaths, and then allow the breath to be natural.

Notice where the breath is felt most pleasantly. Perhaps it's a cool tingling sensation in the back of the throat on the inhale, a warmth on the upper lip on the exhale, or the rise and fall of the chest or belly.

Without trying to change the breath, just notice it. Notice how it naturally changes on its own. The body breathing itself.

Rest your kind attention on the breath, bringing a nonjudgmental awareness and curiosity to the experience of the breath.

When the mind wanders, as it no doubt will, recognize this as a natural process and gently bring the attention back to the breath.

As attention begins to settle a bit, allow your awareness to expand, bringing the attention now to the physical sensations in the body. Take note of the points of contact with the surface beneath you and with the clothing you're wearing.

Scan the body, taking note of any sensations—tingling, vibrating, heat or coolness, heaviness or lightness, throbbing, twitching, pain, even numbness or lack of sensations.

Notice the constellation of sensations as they arise and fall away.

When the mind gets lost in thought, bring the attention back to the physical sensations.

Now that you've become more in tune to the breath and the body, shift the attention to any thoughts and emotions that may be present. Bring your kind attention to these activities of the brain, resting comfortably in knowing that we are not our thoughts or emotions. They are simply products of the mind.

Softly name to yourself the thoughts and emotions that arise. Thinking, planning, worrying, judging. Or content, bored, sad, joy.

Now allow your awareness to expand to the sounds. Without trying to name the sound itself, softly name the quality of the sound. Let it be in the background of your attention. Humming, buzzing, whooshing.

Note to yourself the rise and fall of the sounds.

As we become more aware of our experiences, we begin to cultivate a space where we can hold it all.

Now consider imagining that your mind is as big as the room that you might be in.

Next, expand your mind to be as big as the entire sky. Vast, open, limitless.

Invite an awareness of your entire experience. The breath, the physical sensations, the thoughts and emotions, the sounds. All are like passing clouds, weather, or birds soaring through the sky of your mind. Without getting caught up in the clouds, rest back in awareness as the sky itself.

After a while, you will notice your attention is caught up in a passing cloud. When this happens, gently return to your place as the sky.

Spacious and vast. Open and limitless.
Trust and rest in this realm, as it is your true nature.
Weather changes, birds fly by, and through it all, the mind remains open and aware of it all.

For the last minute of this meditation, take note of what it feels like to inhabit this spacious, receptive presence.

The Three Doors of Liberation

*Nirvana is not a place to get to. It's not something
in the future that we're trying to reach. Nirvana is
available to us right now.*

—Thich Nhat Hanh

Chapter 7: Signlessness

When conditions are sufficient, a cloud transforms into rain, snow, or hail. The cloud has never been born and it will never die. This insight of signlessness and interbeing helps us recognize that all lives continue in different forms.

—Thich Nhat Hanh

"Sometimes I feel like I've outgrown this flowerpot," I explain honestly. "Like I've grown and changed and he's stuck."

It feels mean to say that, but it is real and honest. She nods and sits silently for a moment, taking time to construct a puzzle of who we are and what we need in her mind. It took us a few months to find the right therapist and get an appointment, but here we finally are. I've seen so many therapists in my lifetime, so these first sessions are exhausting but pretty easy for me. I know what they need to hear to get an idea of who we are and what we are looking for. I can recant my childhood trauma with the cool detachment and brevity of a fast food order. This time it includes my partner, which is different.

"What does it feel like to hear Heather say that, Alex?" she asks, appearing genuinely interested.

I fully expect him to be nervous and shut down, so I am surprised to find how open he is.

"It makes me feel scared," he says, looking at her. "I feel like she has changed so much since we first met. She found this Buddhist group, and I'm glad it has been so good for her, but sometimes I worry that she's going to leave me for someone else who is Buddhist, or… just different than me."

I squeeze his hand and look at him, seeing the pain in his eyes. I feel simultaneously sad for how he's feeling and grateful that he's opening up.

"Ah, scared," she emphasized. "You feel scared. Scared of losing her. How does that make you feel, Heather? To hear him be able to name what he's feeling?"

"On the one hand, I feel bad that he feels scared, and on the other, it's such a relief to hear him tell me how he really feels," I say, exhaling out relief.

She nods, and I can see that she already understands the roles we both play in our relationship. I am the one who recognizes my emotions and needs to talk about it, as well as gets frustrated with my partner for shutting down. He is the one who is often disconnected from his emotions and only wants to play the role of a helper, and he grows even more distant when his partner tries to help him.

"I don't want to leave him though," I tell her. Then I turn and look at Alex. "I don't want anyone but you, I promise. I had so much time to think about things on that retreat, and I honestly did take time to consider what a life without you would look like, and I discovered that's not what I want. I still want you."

"Does that bring you comfort, Alex?" she asks him. "Do you believe what she says?"

"Yeah, I do," he says warily, "but I still feel worried about how much she has changed. They're all good changes. It's just … she's not the same person I married. Like, now she's vegan and I'm not, and she's into meditating and Buddhism and I'm not. She is the best mother and cares so much about our kids, and she is always working on herself, and I sometimes wish I could be more like that, but I'm just not like that. I feel like I haven't changed and like I'm getting left behind too sometimes."

"Alex," I say, "we all change. We're constantly changing. Maybe my changes seem bigger on the surface than yours, but you have changed too. The person we married on our wedding day was not the same person the next day, or the next day, or today."

Alex uncomfortably shifts around in his chair.

"I don't like thinking that way," he says. "I married you because I love you, and I still do, but I don't like to think that we're always changing."

"It sounds like you feel scared, Alex," she acknowledges, "scared that change will pull you apart."

"Yeah, I do," he replies.

"If I left you today and married someone who is Buddhist and vegan," I tell him, "that person and I will continue to change, and in ten years from now, we also will not be the same person we married, and I could be in the same situation I am now. People are constantly changing. But even with all the changing that you and I have done, I still want to keep growing and changing with you. Some of my beliefs have changed, like we should not eat animal products, but the core value that belongs to it is compassion for others. And you and I still share that core value. I see how compassionate you are. You are such a good nurse—your patients know how much you care about them. You are a good son—you treat your mother so well and always help her in any way you can. You are an amazing father—you are funny and kind and loving and playful. You are an amazing partner—you left a job to take better care of yourself and your family, you have helped me through so many hard times in my life, and you are here today to work on us. I know you love me."

Love fills every corner of the room, and we allow silence and space for it to linger for a bit.

"What do you both need to feel secure in the relationship?" she asks.

"I need to feel like I'm connecting emotionally with my partner," I say. "I need him to be able to communicate his emotions, so I can help him too, like I'm not the only one who's being helped. When we first met, I had a lot of trauma I hadn't worked through. And I needed him in a way that I don't need him anymore. I feel like I've grown so much, and now I want to feel like I can help him too—like he trusts that I can handle his difficult emotions, like he trusts that helping him helps me."

"Yes, I see," she says. "And Alex, What do you need from Heather?"

"I don't know. Maybe...," he suggests, "maybe just to be more patient with me. Sometimes I feel like I can't do anything right, like she doesn't give me the chance to do things on my own and in my own way. And patience and understanding while I learn how to recognize my emotions and be able to talk about them."

Alex and I share a moment of eye contact that conveys more than we can express in words. He squeezes my hand, and I feel his dedication to us. I feel loved and secure. I feel confident and brave.

"See you next week, right? You two would like a weekly session?" she asks.

So it's set—a weekly session of emotionally focused couple's therapy. Date night! Alex and I joke. This work is good and exhausting.

At the breakfast table one morning, the four of us share waffles and laughs as we begin to plan what we're going to do with our day together. Alex makes a suggestion that he knows the kids won't be able to resist.

"What if we go to the arcade and play games?" he asks.

"Yeah!" the kids yell together.

"Ooh, who's gonna race with me in the go-cart? I'm faster than Daddy," I tease.

"I wanna go with Mommy! I wanna go with Mommy!" Everly shouts.

"Ha! Dad and I are gonna win," Jack says with a cheeky grin.

"Yeah, Jack and I are …" Alex trails off. "Oh my gosh, Jack, I think you lost a tooth!"

Jack's eyes grow big and bright, his mouth widens in a smile, and he covers his mouth.

"Let me see, bud, let me see!" I implore him.

He lowers his hand to reveal a gap-toothed grin, and we all smile and bellow with excitement.

"Jack lost a tooth," we all say. "Jack lost his first tooth!"

Jack covers his mouth and races to the bathroom mirror to see for himself.

"Yeah! I finally lost a tooth!" he announces and laughs.

Alex and I smile, both in awe of how quickly it seems our kids are growing up.

"Wait," I say. "Where is the tooth, Jack?"

Everyone starts searching on the table, under the table, in the leftover waffle on his plate.

"I kind of feel like I noticed him bite down on something hard while he was chewing…" I say, trying to hide my mild disgust.

"What?" Jack asks.

"You swallowed it, bud," Alex says.

Jack's eyes widen, and a look of fear comes across his face.

"What?" he asks. "Am I gonna be okay?"

"Yeah, buddy," I say with a gentle laugh. "You're gonna be okay."

"You'll just poop the tooth out later," Alex breaks the ice.

Jack and Everly laugh hysterically. And once again, all is well.

Oh, the poop jokes. They never fail to make them laugh. I hope the kids don't make jokes like this at school.

"You're growing up, man," I tell him. "That's awesome! We'll just put a note under your pillow for the tooth fairy and explain what happened. It'll be okay."

"Okay," Jack says with relief.

It never ceases to amaze me how quickly my children grow and change. The days are slow and the years are fast, they say. How true that is. I reflect on the day I was dancing with baby Jack in the kitchen, when he was about a week old. Alex and I had cranked the music up and danced and sang to our firstborn. I admired his tiny and awkwardly moving arms, the distinct expressions on his scrunched-up face, and I laughed out loud—that's all you can do when you're filled with that kind of joy.

There are times I've condemned the quick passage of time, realizing how this moment I have with this version of him is the last time I will have. And there are other times when I have willed the hours, the days to pass, to a time when I wouldn't be needed so much. But here we all are orbiting the sun at the same rate. None of us can stop it, none of us can speed it up, and all we have is this exact moment in time.

I look at him now, recognizing that while he is still "Jack," the child I gave birth to and have spent almost every single day with since, he's not exactly the same. Which, on all accounts, is very clear by the loss of his tooth today. But truthfully, this change has always been happening right in front of us, and yet we always cling to the idea of who someone "is."

"You're so big, Jack!" Everly tells him, knowing very well how much he loves to hear that.

He walks over to her and puts his arm around her. "I love being your brother," he says to her.

"I love being your girl," Everly sweetly replies.

Alex and I share a glance that implies both "How sweet!" and "Don't make a big deal of it in front of them."

"Who's ready to go play games and race go-karts?!" Alex asks.

"Me!" two kids shout, syrupy fingers thrown up, reaching for the sky.

"Let's go wash our hands and get dressed. Come with me, Evie Devie," I say to my spunky daughter.

I go to her bedroom to pick out an outfit for her while she washes up. I hear a fluttering, flapping sound and worriedly scan the room. Then it dawns on me.

"Everly!" I shout. "Alex, Jack come here! Everly's butterflies have come out of their cocoons!"

They all race in to see as I lower the butterfly habitat to the floor. The butterflies' wings are colorful, crinkly, and small.

"Wow, cool!" the kids shout.

I grab the manual that came with the butterfly kit, a bit confused and worried by the appearance of their wings.

"Oh," I say, "it says here that when the butterflies first emerge from the chrysalis, their wings will be damp and wrinkly. They need to dry out for a day or so before we can release them!"

This was such a great gift for Everly, my little purple butterfly.

Butterflies are one of Everly's favorite things in the world, which is very fitting. She's always flitting about, she's beautiful to watch, and I've always had this feeling that as soon as she's able, she's going to fly away on some great adventure.

The kids waste no time expending all their energy at the arcade, and Alex and I barely manage to keep up. We race go-karts (I do win, by the way) and play Giant Hungry Hungry Hippos and a round of putt-putt golf. They seem more interested in hopping around the obstacles on the green and "helping" Alex and me by picking up our golf balls and moving them for us, but we have fun.

On the drive home, Alex tells me his latest advancement in his woodworking. He's recently started selling them online and is currently working on building his own website.

"I did my 'About Me' page on my website," he explains, "and instead of writing 'I *am* a nurse', I wrote, 'I *work* as a nurse'."

"Oh yeah?" I look at him, curious and eager for a longer explanation.

"Yeah," he goes on. "Ever since we talked about how we cause ourselves suffering by attaching to our labels, I've really noticed how true that is for me, like in being able to say, 'I'm an ICU nurse' and stuff."

"Cool, honey," I say, smiling. "I'm glad that's been helpful for you. It has helped me so much too. You'll have to show me the website when we get home."

"Yeah, totally," he agrees. "It's so cool but also weird selling my woodworking now. I still don't really feel like I can call myself a true woodworker, like I haven't earned it yet."

"Oh, honey," I reassure him, "you've earned it. You *are* a woodworker. You should totally call yourself that now."

We both immediately sense the irony in the turn of our conversation and laugh out loud.

"Or not," I say.

I reflect on a conversation I had a while ago with my primary mindfulness teacher, Noah, about my struggle with identifying as a "good" or "bad" mom. He made a simple, yet profound point that the qualities of a "good" mother are ambiguous and subject to change based on time period, societal norms and expectations, beliefs, and mental conditioning. Basically, a "good" mother is not something that can be pinpointed, measured, or objectified. A "good" mother is an idea, a concept that is constantly shifting, changing, and not obtainable as a concrete accolade.

I've noticed how over the past couple of years, my negative self-talk has lessened or, at the very least, I'm less likely to believe it. I still make mistakes. Lots of them. I yell sometimes, I can be impatient, I can hold unrealistic expectations of my children just for them to bite me in the butt. And when I make these mistakes, and my internal voice says, "See, you're a bad mom," I can put my hand on my heart and say back to myself, "Ah. I feel guilty. I'm not going to let myself believe I'm a bad mom, though. I made a mistake, and I will continue to work on myself and do better." And you know what? I feel like I've had the most personal growth since I've stopped condemning myself for my mistakes. Shame doesn't win.

I read books to the kids that evening after their bedtime routines. I tuck in Jack and kiss him on the top of the head.

"Good night, buddy," I tell him. "I love you. Have sweet dreams, and I'll see you in the morning!"

"Good night, Mom," he replies.

Everly does acrobats to climb into her bed, as usual. I tuck her in just as she insists, purple blanket first, hearts on top, and then the sheet and blankets.

"Everly, wasn't that so amazing seeing the butterflies today?" I ask her. I then continue, "It's so cool that they literally started out as caterpillars, built a cocoon around themselves, then emerged something completely different!"

"Yeah… ," she says, appearing a bit uneasy and distracted.

"You okay, sweetheart?" I ask her. "What's wrong?"

"Mommy," she says with concern on her face, "I don't want to poop a tooth out."

It takes all of me to keep my composure and not burst out laughing.

"Oh, honey," I console her, "that's not going to happen to you. You're not going to swallow your teeth."

The tiny wrinkles in her face relax, and she smiles, just a bit.

"Okay, goodnight, Mommy!" she announces.

"Goodnight, my little butterfly," I say, as I tuck her in and kiss her goodnight.

****

The three doors of liberation are profound truths rooted in the Buddhist tradition that, once realized, lead to liberation from fear and suffering. They include emptiness, signlessness, and aimlessness, and they all lead us to a path that liberates us from unnecessary suffering. "Sign" in this context refers to a presentation or object of our perception. Without a deep understanding of emptiness, interdependence, and impermanence, we will not be able to see beyond signs as they are presented to us. "I" as a separate thing is a sign, but where there is a sign, there is deception. Emptiness teaches me that "I" is a sign, a representation of all the causes and conditions that have made me "me."

Where we see form, we see signs. Where we see signs, we assign labels. Navigating throughout our lives and through the world without labels would be difficult if not impossible, but the manner in which we relate to these labels can drastically make a difference in the amount of contentment we find in this life.

Eating breakfast, I see a lot of signs. I drink coffee out of my ceramic coffee mug, and I recognize "coffee mug" as a sign. The coffee mug is an object of my perception, and labeling it as so allows me to communicate to others my wants and needs. I may say to my partner, "Darling, can you please bring me a cup of coffee?" My partner needs to be able to conceive of the concept of a cup, the sign "cup," in order to be able to fulfill my request. I need to be able to recognize these signs to navigate through my life, but they are just that: signs.

Labels can serve us well, as long as we recognize they are signs and not attach ourselves to them. If I am ill, I need to be able to find proper health care. I need to be able to know and comprehend the label "Doctor" so I can get the help I need. If my car breaks down and I am in need of assistance, I need to recognize the label of "auto mechanic" so that I can get my vehicle repaired. If I want to learn something new and need guidance, I need to be able to perceive "teacher" and seek out a guide. Signs are very important in our ability to care for ourselves and navigate through our lives.

Trouble lies ahead, however, when we don't recognize the labels are just signs, when we are caught in the illusion that the object of our perception is its own permanent and separate thing. The coffee mug can skillfully be referred to as a cup so that I can communicate my needs and wants. It is important that I am able to recognize, however, that "cup" is just a sign and not get attached to "cup" in this form. Say I accidentally drop the cup on the hard ground, and it shatters into multiple pieces. Has it stopped being "cup?" What if I glue it back together as best as I can? Is it "cup" again? What if I rearrange the shattered pieces into a beautiful mosaic and hang it as art? Is it no longer "cup?"

Signlessness teaches me that the cup is not gone, that it has taken a new formation. "Cup" was just a sign to begin with, a recognizable object that I used to drink from. "Cup" was made of non-cup elements, configured in such a way that I was able to perceive this sign, "cup."

Anywhere I see signs, I see the potential for confusion, deception. Rock, tree, car, house, person—these are all signs, all subject to change, all connected to each other, none as separate or permanent as they appear. It is not necessary for us to abandon the use of labels in our daily lives in order to gain freedom; we just need to have a more skillful relationship with them.

So much of the unskillful labeling we do is how we assign labels to ourselves and others. Some of the labels we use for people are desirable, while others we avoid. Either way, these labels that seem to serve us can hurt us, even the labels we strive for.

We begin assigning labels to signs we recognize as young children, in order to be able to understand and safely navigate the world around us. One of the earliest potential problem labels children run into in their early experiences is "good guys" versus "bad guys." Such a common game played among children can begin to set a precedent for the desire to categorize people into definable, rigid groups.

As parents, we can unfortunately, but understandably, feed into this concept of "good guys" versus "bad guys" in order to protect our children from potential harm. The problem this creates, however, is that children then begin to process people's worth and value based on a label we have assigned, as they lack the ability to separate the person from the behavior.

I've never even used the term "bad guys," but perhaps while playing with school mates, my son has learned that term and uses it in his play. He asked me recently, "Mommy, why are bad guys bad?"

I asked him, "Well, what do you think is a bad guy?"

To which he responded, "Like someone who steals something."

I asked him what kinds of things he imagines people might steal.

He said, "Like food." I questioned why someone might steal food, to which he replied, "Because they're hungry."

Obviously, the harmful behaviors humans may have go way beyond stealing food when they can't afford it. In this situation, however, I felt compelled to help my son break his framework of "bad guy" and help him use creativity and compassion to imagine why people might do the things they do, and not feel so attached to the label of "good" or "bad." I then asked my son if he ever does anything bad, to which he honestly and shamefully responded, "Yes." I comforted him and told him we all do bad things sometimes, even Mommy and Daddy. I am not a perfect parent, and every time I make a mistake with my children, like losing my temper and yelling, I acknowledge my mistake and apologize. I asked my son if he thought I was a bad person or if he was a bad person, and he said, "No."

I followed up by asking, "So, if people sometimes do bad things, does that make them bad?"

Looking perplexed, he said, "No, it doesn't."

This may seem like such a simple, straightforward exercise, but even as adults, we tend to lack the creativity and awareness to see beyond the labels we've assigned ourselves and others. We fit people into little boxes and assign fixed characteristics that we take to be true.

When we can only recognize signs as the labels we've ascribed, we are disregarding the impermanent and interdependent nature of all beings. Even the term "criminal" evokes a certain quality of characteristics, a certain stigma to arise in our minds of what we perceive "criminal" to be.

When we comprehend the label we have given someone as the limitations to their existence, we fail to see their true nature and make harmful assumptions. The moment we label someone as a criminal and put them in prison, we create a situation where there is a separation of "them" versus "me" and lack creativity and insight when it comes to the way we think about that person.

The term "criminal" may evoke thoughts of someone who "is bad" and is solely to blame for the harmful actions they made. If we were able to see beyond the label, we'd be able to have a whole new perspective on the individual. Instead of saying, "This person is a criminal because they committed a crime, therefore they must be punished," we would look beyond the labels and observe with contemplation and curiosity.

We are all interdependent in nature, as is the "criminal." Using the lens of interdependence, we could ask more skillful questions. We would be interested in the "criminal's" upbringing, what kind of childhood they had. Were they cared for and did they feel loved? Did they have a healthy attachment to their parents? Were they shown compassion and understanding, and were they taught how to handle difficult emotions? Were all of their physical and emotional needs met as a child? Was there any violence in the home? Did they grow up living in poverty? Was there any substance abuse in the home they grew up in? We can look at some of their demographics, such as: Has their ethnicity played a role in how they are perceived in the world and limited their ability to live a safe life? What kind of neighborhood did this person grow up in? Was there a lot of crime? We can look at the culture they are living in. What is the political situation? Is there a lot of unrest? What is the norm of behavior in the area this person is from? What are the current societal pressures as far as success is concerned? What is their employment status, and if unemployed, what are the employment opportunities like in the area they are from? This is certainly not an exhaustive list, but it gives us the perspective of criminal behavior from an interdependent perspective.

We need some version of social order so that we can all live safely. There is a lot of false reassurance we give ourselves, however, by imprisoning so many people who have committed crimes, because it allows us to ignore the entire picture. The "criminal" is not what it appears to be. "Criminal" is not one person who, independent of all other things, committed a crime. "Criminal" is everything—the society, the culture, the environment; it is us.

The belief that we can draw conclusions about people based on the labels we've given them is harmful, and also simply not an accurate picture. The nature of interdependence is such that everything gives rise to everything else, so if we want to truly understand who someone is, we can't look just at the person we see before us, the sign or label we have appointed.

What would this "criminal" be in another context? Are they also a mother or father? How else would we define them and how else would they define themselves? If they atone for the crime they committed and they go on to function more positively in their society, are they still a "criminal?" At which point, did they stop being a "criminal?" The answer is difficult to find because there is no true answer. Not only are we not interdependent in nature, but we are also impermanent. I am not the same person I was ten years ago, or even yesterday. The so-called "criminal" is not the exact same person they were as when they committed the crime.

As the Diamond Sutra in Buddhist teachings describes, where there are signs, there is deception. When we believe the sign is its own, separate, fixed thing, we lack creativity and curiosity and miss the whole picture. By labeling people who commit crimes as criminals, it gives us a sense of security because we can tell ourselves, "The criminal is in prison," but the criminal is not just the person—it is everything that makes the person who they are. It is also easier to blame a single person for a crime than fix a broken system, so labeling criminals as such can also be seen as scapegoating a much bigger, more complicated problem.

So many of the signs we see that we assign labels to are because they make us feel safe. I understand who I am, and I feel the need to understand who you are. But the reality of who we are is far more complex than a set of behaviors we've engaged in, the career we choose, the political party we vote for, our sexuality, or our gender identity and expression.

When we are living our lives, experiencing and interpreting each moment as it arises, we are all blind men touching an elephant. What may appear to be so clearly one thing, when we contemplate it from all other angles, our idea of the object we perceive may change.

While it is necessary for us to use some labels in order to be able to navigate our lives at ease, the manner in which we relate to these labels is extremely important. If we are unable to see beyond our own personal labels, it can cause us great suffering. It's clear why labels such as "bad guy" or "criminal" can be problematic. People who have been ascribed those labels may feel little to no power in changing. They may cause themselves great suffering by only blaming themselves or react by blaming everyone else. Either way, these undesirable labels leave little motivation for the capacity to change, to do better.

The labels we desire and actively seek out can also cause us great suffering. Biologically primed for fear of exclusion, we try to inflate ourselves and strategically position ourselves in our communities to be perceived exactly the way we wish to. We consider our labels to be extremely important, so much so that we would fight to defend them. We over identify with our achievements and our perceived failures, both of which can cause us distress.

By over-identifying with our labels and achievements, we begin to believe that the labels we've given ourselves truly define who we are, as if we are a permanent, fixed being. We use our labels as ways to find others "like us" and exclude others who are "not like us." I am white, I am American, I am a nurse, I am a mother, I am a wife, I am a yogi, I am vegan. I tell myself that these labels are who I am, and this naturally lends to me attaching to them as part of my identity.

When I decided to "be vegan," it initially caused me a lot of emotional turmoil. My partner and my children still eat meat, and I would tell myself, "I am vegan and my family is omnivorous. I am now something they are not." I experienced a lot of guilt and sadness, and I felt like I had alienated myself from my family. I felt like this life choice somehow made me less like them, less connected to them. I knew they still loved me and accepted me, but somehow I felt like I had betrayed them by "becoming something" they were not.

It disturbed me so much that I ended up giving up veganism for a few months, but during those months, I was also suffering because I felt like I was not being true to myself. I felt like no matter what decision I made, to be vegan or not to be vegan, I would not be happy.

I then began to observe with curiosity why veganism was so important to me. During this introspection, I discovered that my drive toward veganism was deeply rooted in my value of compassion for others. I feel compassionate toward others, in advocating for those who need a voice. I then contemplated what are the shared values that my partner and I share together and what I wanted to share with our children.

I had met my spouse when we were in nursing school; we were in the same cohort and spent much of our early time with each other studying various diseases together. I recall being drawn to his compassionate qualities, his desire to help others heal and relieve their suffering. He chose nursing as a profession because of his passion for helping others. I recognized that moment that we both valued compassion for others.

Our shared value, compassion, has driven my personal belief that we should not consume animal products. While he at this time does not share that same belief, we still share that core value of compassion. I discovered that we are still deeply connected to one another.

I realized there was an issue when I thought of myself as "being vegan," opposed to "living a vegan lifestyle." This seemingly subtle distinction makes a world of a difference when it comes to our connection to others. The moment I tell myself "I am" something, it creates a distinction between what "I am" and what someone else "is" or "is not."

The only thing that changed when I began to feel better about being vegan was how I attached myself to the label of veganism. For simplicity and convenience purposes, I tell others such as food service employees that I "am" vegan, but my internal mental framework reflects something different. Internally, I don't cling to the label of "being vegan," and instead, I tell myself I avoid all use and consumption of animal products.

The separation of my core identity and the choices I make was liberating. It gave me the freedom to be flexible with my identity. It is interesting that we identify with the choices we make. Since I used to not "be vegan" and now I "am," does that mean I am not myself anymore? Who am I? Is there a stable sense of self? Is there a core "me"? Who am "I"? Am I more "me" now than I was before I was vegan? Or was I me then just as much as I am me now?

This confusion stems from the attachment we have to a fixed, permanent self. I likely would not have experienced this discomfort had I not had this unskillful attachment to the idea of who "I was" and who I am supposed to be.

I know that who I am is not just what I see looking back at me in the mirror, the credentials after my name, or any of the other achievements I have accomplished or the mistakes I have made. Being human, I will still inevitably become attached to new identities, such as being the person who is unattached to my identities. The difference now, however, is that I have an awareness of the labels I am giving myself and continue to observe myself as a dynamic, impermanent, and interdependent being with an open curiosity. I continue to learn about myself by cultivating a beginner's mind, recognizing that "I" can never be clearly defined.

****

Awareness Exercise:

1. Begin an elemental meditation practice.

    Elemental meditations are a powerful tool to reconnect you to your true nature by reconnecting to the elements. The purpose of this elemental meditation is to embody our connection to the earth and identify less with our labels. If possible, find a comfortable space outside to meditate for this guided meditation.

    If you're new to meditating outdoors, you might discover more distractions than when meditating indoors. Continue to use your breath as an anchor (or your anchor of choice) to the present moment when you become lost in thought.

Guided Elemental Meditation:

Once you find a comfortable place to meditate outside, take a moment to find a comfortable position. It can be sitting on a cushion or bench on the ground or on a chair. The closer you can get to the earth and the most direct connection you can have to the earth, the better.

Begin by taking a moment to notice your surroundings. Once you feel comfortable, let your eyes gently close or rest half open in a slight downward gaze and begin to rest in the present moment.

Consider taking in a few deep cleansing breaths, then allow your breath to become natural. Rest your attention on wherever you most easily detect the breath or wherever it is most pleasant.

Today we are going to meditate on the four elements that we share in common with the earth. These are the earth element, the air element, the water element, and the fire element.

Beginning with the earth element, let's tune in to the way this element manifests in our bodies.

Find a posture that is upright, with the spine erect, grounded, connected to the earth. Sense into the density, the heaviness, the solidity of your body.

Feel yourself rooted to the ground. Whether it's your buttocks, your feet, or whatever is making contact with the ground, allow yourself to feel deeply rooted and connected to the earth.

The density and solidity of your bones are made stronger by calcium, the same element that is abundant in the earth. Sense your connection to the earth element.

The earth element nourishes our bodies through the plants that we eat, and one day when we die, our bodies will return to the earth.

We are not separate from the earth.

Sense the earth element inside and outside your body, and the flow of energy between the two.

Now we'll tune into the air element. Begin by sensing the air element inside your body. Notice the air as it fills your lungs, entering through your nostrils. Maybe you notice a cool sensation in the back of your throat as you inhale, the expansion of your lungs down into your belly as the air fills your lungs, and the movement of air back out of your body as you exhale.
Air moves in… and out.
In… and out.

Now sense into the air element of the earth in the breeze, the wind, the still air. The trees, the plants, and algae—all capturing the carbon dioxide that we exhale and releasing oxygen that we inhale.
The flow of air between you and the earth.

Now tune into the water element.

Begin by sensing the water element present in your body.

Your body is made of 60 percent water. It is flowing through your veins, providing fluid in your joints, your sweat and saliva.
Now sense into the water element in the earth. Water is present in the clouds, the rain, the rivers, the lakes, the oceans, the humidity.

Your body is mostly made up of the water that you drink daily, which likely comes from the land that you live in.

You are not separate from the land.

Now sense into the fire element.

Begin with how the fire element manifests in your body.

Sense into the heat of your breath as you exhale on your upper lip and the heat in your belly.

Now sense into the fire element of the earth. The fire of the sun. Sense the heat on your skin from the sun.

The sun gives life to the plants that grow so that we may nourish our bodies.

The fire element is present in ourselves and in the earth.

Now allow yourself to be aware of the flow of these four elements inside and outside of your body.

The solidity and density of the earth element, the breath, the water in our bodies, and the heat.

As American Tibetan Buddhist Pema Chodron said, "Our true nature is like a precious jewel: although it may be temporarily buried in mud, it remains completely brilliant and unaffected. We simply have to uncover it."
We spend so much of our time trying to prove ourselves and others that we are who we say we are. We spend a lot of energy constructing and defending the stories we create about who we are and denying the stories we don't wish to be true.

The freedom is in knowing that we can let all of the stories go.

This presence we've cultivated here is what's real. We are not separate from the earth. Our true nature lies here, in the elements.

When you are ready, allow your eyes to open.

Chapter 8: Emptiness

The unnecessary suffering we experience has more to do with how we see things than with what we see.

—Noah Rasheta

The kids have been taking turns being sick lately, so there's been a lot of missed school days, extra snuggles, screen time, and snotty rags around the house.

It would be nice if they could agree to be sick at the same time, so we could get this over and done with.

I make myself laugh out loud.

"What?" Alex asks, a little grumpily.

"Nothing, I just had a funny thought," I say.

Monday and Tuesday mornings are my mornings alone. The kids are both in school, and I get to have my "me" time. Alex is off Wednesdays while I work, and those mornings are his alone time. By some strange coincidence, it seems like the kids keep getting sick and needing to stay home on Wednesdays.

I have recently started a YouTube channel about mindfulness, and that's what I often use my "me" time for. Otherwise, I'm working on my mindfulness teacher program. Alex usually uses his time for woodworking, and he's currently behind on some orders.

I can see the exhaustion in his eyes. I imagine he is physically tired and wishing he had more time to go do woodworking. We always take turns putting the kids to bed; that way one parent gets to "check out" early and get some extra rest. Tonight is his turn to put the kids down, and as much as I would love to turn in early this evening and snuggle up on the couch with a book, I sense his needs are greater than mine right now.

"Hey, honey," I tell him, "Why don't I put the kids to bed tonight? I can see how tired you are… And I recognize how you haven't had much time to yourself lately."

"Really?" he says, his face immediately displaying relief. "That would be awesome. Thank you."

These past few months, I've begun to really notice how extending kindness and compassion to Alex, to my children, and to others fills me up as well. I have this sense of the boundlessness of my existence. When I hurt you, I hurt myself. When I take care of you, I am taking care of myself. We are interconnected.

"Ooh! Let me show you what happened with my YouTube short I posted yesterday," I excitedly declare.

I pull up the most recent video and play it for him. Jack recognizes the sound and comes running up, laughing.

"This one's good, huh, buddy?" I ask him.

He laughs, and Alex tells me how good and creative it is.

"Look at all the comments," I direct Alex.

"Good ones?" he asks.

"Yes, thankfully," I answer.

I'm still trying to figure out if social media is a skillful outlet for me for teaching mindfulness. My original thoughts were: well, it would be nice to have some passive income, and I like the idea of making these teachings more accessible. I'm noticing, however, how tricky it is to be mindful with teaching mindfulness on social media. I can sense my inflation and deflation of my "self" based on how people are interacting with my posts. I feel myself start to value and devalue myself based on the types of comments I'm getting. I'm using a platform to teach about mindfulness, and for people to be able to find me I have to brand myself, while internally trying to un-brand myself. So here I am, trying to teach others how to cultivate a healthier view of "self" while feeding my ego. I recognize, however, that even the praises don't belong only to me. They belong to my teacher, my ancestors, my family, and all the conditions that have brought me to this place with these insights.

Life is complicated. I'm going to have to learn and relearn these lessons over and over again.

Jack smiles at me, and I caress his hair, his long beautiful tresses chopped off. A recent visit to the hair salon resulted in his choice to make a dramatic change to his hair, seemingly influenced by his idea of what was "cool" from the other kids at school.

Oh my dear child. Even I cannot prevent you from experiencing the suffering that comes with chasing the unreachable perfect self-image. All I can do is always make you feel wholly accepted at home, for whoever you choose to be.

"What's for dinner tonight, Mommy?" Jack asks, a worried look on his face.

"… Kielbasa, rice, and veggies," I say with hesitation.

His pickiness with food has not gotten any easier. He often adamantly refuses to eat dinner, opting to go to bed hungry. I recognize anxiety arising in me every evening at dinner time. I often feel angry when he refuses to eat, but I recognize that fear is fueling that anger. I worry about my children, and I want them to be happy and healthy.

"Ugh, I hate rice and veggies!" Jack exclaims.

We sit at the dinner table, and Jack refuses to eat, pushing his plate around and demanding something else to eat. Everly mimics him. I can feel the anger rising up inside me, as I attempt to gently coax them to try the kielbasa or anything on their plates.

"No! I won't eat it!" Jack announces.

"Well, that's all that's for dinner!" I angrily snap back.

I reflect on the length of time this problem has been going on. Everyone says, "children can be picky," but instead of this feeling comforting, it feels dismissive. I'm his parent, and I feel in my gut like something more is going on. I reflect on his earliest experiences with eating. I remember his tiny late preterm body attempting to stay awake long enough to finish a feeding. I remember my body barely able to keep up with the milk supply and my anxiety about it. I recall the day he was rushed to the emergency room, after we'd given him a bottle of soy-based formula because my milk supply was dropping.

"He has a rare food allergy," they'd said. "But to all of what we can't know without him trying the food."

It was less than reassuring for two new parents who felt helpless and just wanted to feed their child. Every time I fed him as a baby, I was riddled with anxiety. I tried to mask it, to paint a smile on my face and hide my fear for his sake, but I'm sure he sensed it.

Jack's struggle with food wasn't his fault, or my fault, or anyone's fault. The issue arose from all the causes and conditions that led to this. There is no one to point the finger at, to blame, to unleash my anger on.

"I'm sorry, guys," I confess. "I'm just worried about you. I want you to be healthy and grow, and you need food to do that. I'm sorry I yelled. I will do better next time. I love you."

They both take a few bites, and that is that. My apology and recognition didn't magically fix the issue with food, but it did help how I'm relating to the pain of it.

No one is to blame for his struggle with food. It doesn't mean I am a bad mother.

I still experience guilt and remorse whenever I make a mistake, but I'm not locked in shame anymore. I can see that there are causes and conditions that have led to all my triggers. My body still carries with it the metaphorical scars of the traumatic experiences I witnessed and experienced as a child and young adult. I can see how I am tied to my ancestors, in all its grim and glory. I can see how my scars are their scars, how the pain they caused me was a result of a bunch of causes and conditions as well. I can see beyond their hurtful actions and recognize their inherent goodness.

I recognize how the person I call myself today is not the same person as I was a couple of years ago and how Noah Rasheta's teachings on Buddhism live through me. I acknowledge how the mindfulness program I am in right now is changing me, living through me, and how I am not separate from the teachings. I know that when I obtain the new label of Mindfulness Meditation Teacher, it is not just "I" that will be sitting in that chair teaching. It will be my teachers, my ancestors, my family, my culture, and the river. There is no "I" that exists outside of everyone and everything else. My existence is dependent on everyone and everything else.

Where is the bad mom? I see a history of ancestors with trauma and a history of poor decision-making. I see the struggle of those ancestors to do better. I see suffering, and I see growth. I see the culture of that mother, the land she grew up on, and all the other circumstances and events that influenced her. So, where is she? Where is the bad mother?

The next day after breakfast, the four of us pile into the car for our annual leaf peeping excursion. A short hike in Golden Gate Canyon State Park reveals to us an array of colorful leaves decorating the trees and the forest floor. The kids run ahead and slow down when called back, again run ahead, then slow down when called. I intentionally take each moment to take in my surroundings, noting the sound of the wind through the aspen tree leaves, appreciating the dance of light through the trees, and soaking in the comforting smell of Autumn.

I think about my mother. I wonder if she's finding herself delightfully in the midst of a colorful forest as well. I hope so; I hope she is finding joy. I hope she is discovering a love and acceptance that she was never shown to her by her parents. My existence is inextricably tied to her. Like these colorful quaking aspens, I am bound to my mother. My healing is her healing, is our healing. The burden of anger I have carried has been released like the golden leaves beneath my feet, leaving space for something new to grow. I vow to continue to water the seeds of compassion and understanding every day.

We find a giant rock at the top to rest on and enjoy the view. Everly points out a fallen tree and asks with curiosity what happened to it.

"I don't know, honey," Alex tells her. "Maybe it was sick, or maybe there was a big windstorm that knocked it over."

"But," she asks with concern, "what will happen to it now? Will it go back into the earth? Will it make a new tree?"

"Maybe," I reassure her. "Maybe it will turn into another tree. And you are right; it will go back into the earth and help create something new. Just because one day we won't be able to see the tree anymore doesn't mean it's not there. It's just become something new."

"But the tree can't change on its own," Alex continues. "It needs the help of the sun, the rain, the air, the dirt beneath it."

"So really," I tell her, "When you see a tree, you're also seeing the seeds, the soil, a cloud, the rain, and the sun."

"Oh," she says, looking curious and perplexed. "So it doesn't die?"

"Not really," I tell her. "Kind of. But I think it's more accurate to say that it's changing form."

We sit on that rock for almost an hour, each moment noticing something new—the moss in the cracks of the rock, a cool climbing spot, the place with the best view. The clouds cover the sun, and we get a chill. Then they part, and the sun warms us again. Finally, a large cloud comes in, and it looks like rain is coming.

"Time to head back," Alex suggests.

We head back down the mountain, which always makes me more nervous than going up.

"Slow down, kids. I don't want you to slip!" I plead.

To no avail, they run, and they trip. They're upset for a bit, then get up and run again. They find long sticks and put them between their legs.

"We're witches!" they declare, and they cackle in the most humorous way.

Alex and I share an "aren't they adorable?" look and trail behind the two little witches all the way back to our van.

On our windy mountain drive home, I share with Alex how I've noticed that I don't seem to be burdened with the idea of being a "bad" mom anymore.

"Yeah, now that you say it," he concurs, "I haven't heard you mention that to me in a while."

"The thought still comes up," I explain, "but not as often, and I don't really believe it anymore. It's like now I'm able to examine my thoughts instead of 'being' them."

He nods. This has been a major part of our lives, fixing the parts of me that feel broken, confused, and lacking. I by no means have transcended self-criticism, but I notice a relief from the old perpetual cycle of berating myself.

"I think I actually used to believe that shaming myself would make me better. But it made me feel frozen and powerless," I say out loud. "But I actually feel like I've had the most personal growth now that I've stopped believing those thoughts."

"That's good, honey," he agrees, smiling.

Shame was what I learned growing up, and it has failed me. There's no blame here, as shame is probably what my parents learned as well. But I'm ready to ditch it and shift courses. I want my children to feel remorse and regret for mistakes they make, as I do, but not shame. I don't want them to believe they are inadequate, defective, or flawed. And I can only teach what I know—so starting with teaching myself is crucial.

"I'm so glad the kids haven't been sick in almost a whole week," I say.

Alex weaves around the tight corners on the one-lane mountain roads.

"Me too," he says. "Maybe we're finally in the clear for a while. I feel like we've paid our sick dues."

I agree, chuckling.

"Uhhh … Daddy," Everly whimpers, "I'm going to fwow up."

****

We experience our lives through the lens of "I" interacting with "everyone else." We navigate our world through perceiving everything as fixed, permanent things that are separate from us and other things. Things appear to happen "to us" in a way that separates us from others. We discern every form, object, and individual as its own separate self and operate our lives as if we do not all have a shared existence.

We see a chair and only see the form of chair, but when we contemplate everything that makes the chair a chair, we see that the chair exists only because of so much else happening in the universe. When we look at a chair, if we truly see the chair, we will see so much more than just the still image of "chair" in front of us. We will see the trees, from which the wood was sourced to build it; we will see the sun and the clouds and the rain, which nourished that tree and helped it grow; we will see the soil and the landscape that the tree called home as it grew; we will see the mycelium, the underground network that supported the tree's growth; we will see the logger who cut the tree down and the logger's parents who raised them; we will see the truck driver who delivered the wood to the factory; we will see the woodworker who planed and milled the wood for use; we will see the store clerk who sold us the chair.

Nothing and no one exist separately from everything else; everything is connected, and nothing inherently has its own separate identity. This concept is known as emptiness in Buddhist teachings, another part of the three doors of liberation.

Thich Nhat Hanh illuminated emptiness by describing it as "interbeing"— the prefix "inter," meaning reciprocally or together, combined with the suffix "being." The term "interbeing" illuminates our inability to be just ourselves alone, since our existence is contingent on everything else. Anattā, or no-self, is the Buddhist term for our interconnected existence with all of life. All things are empty of a separate self, and all things exist because they are interconnected with everything else around it. It is not to say that the chair and the tree are the exact same thing, but that the chair cannot exist without the tree. Everything is interconnected, coexisting in a way that gives life to everything else.

When people first hear the word "emptiness," it may evoke thoughts about things having no meaning, no purpose, and no worth, but that is not what is being expressed here. Emptiness in the Buddhist tradition is not to say that we are nothing or empty of meaning but to say that in fact we are everything. My existence is possible because of emptiness, because of my interconnectedness to everything else. I am not nothing. I am everything.

The existence of emptiness is not a spiritual belief we can choose whether or not to buy into; it's scientific fact. Nothing in the world exists independently of all other things. We are all existing as we are because of everything and everyone else.

I exist because of my mother and my father, and they exist because of their parents. It is also conceivable that "I" existed before I was born, as an embryo, and even before that, with my DNA tied to my ancestors.

I am my mother and my father, and I am their parents.

I am connected to the land and everything that sustained the life of my ancestors. I am connected to the clouds that gave rain, which gave rise to the food my ancestors ate.

I am the food that sustained my parents.

Since the day of my birth and every day since then, I have been changing. At the end of May in the late 1980s, my mother gave birth to a baby girl. She named her Heather, a name she had chosen years before. She took Heather home from the hospital and raised her and cared for her. She saw her go through each developmental stage and grow and change every day. The baby she brought home from the hospital, however, is not the exact same person as she is today.

Ever since my birth, the cells that have formed my body that I have called "me" have died, and new cells have been formed. The blood that pumped through my arteries and veins in my body on the day I was born has since died and been replaced by new blood cells multiple times. My skin cells are continuously renewing themselves, the face I see in the mirror is never exactly the same as the day before. This image of myself, this concept I call "I," is not as permanent as I experience it.

I cannot even accurately say that I am completely separate from everything around me. Roughly 55 percent of my body is made of water. I currently live in Fort Collins, Colorado, and my drinking supply comes from the Poudre River and Horsetooth Reservoir. More than half of my body is filled with local water sources, and those sources of water exist because of the clouds, rain, and mountain streams emerging from Rocky Mountain National Park. The same water that fills my body also fills the body of the deer that drinks from the river, the body of the trout that swims through the lake.

I am the river and the lake.

My lungs repeatedly fill with oxygen, supplied to me by the plants around me. The oxygen enters my bloodstream and hitches a ride on the back of a red blood cell, visiting all the organs and tissues in my body. I exhale carbon dioxide, and the trees capture it and transform it into energy for themselves and in turn give me oxygen back.

I am the plants that surround me.

I walk each day as I live my life, each and every step I take changing the earth beneath my feet. I walk the same favorite trails with my partner and children, and each time we visit the trail is different. The earth is creating me, and I am creating the earth. Without everything else, there is no "me." The existence of "myself" is contingent upon everything else in the universe.

In the same way that I "am" everything, I also "am" nothing. When difficult feelings arise, I may say to myself, "I am angry," but who is the I that is angry? My feelings come and go like the passing wind, so how can my emotions be something that I am? It is probably more accurate to say that I *feel* angry rather than I *am* angry. There is no denying my emotions—I can feel them, and the feeling is real, but that doesn't make it who I am.

Which version of "me" is the real "'me?" Is it the "me" when I've had a good night's sleep and a decent breakfast? While I do carry some consistent characteristics and tendencies, I can't truthfully say I am always the same. Depending on the situation and so many other factors, similar events may trigger a different response from me.

My education does not even belong entirely to me; it is not mine. We've already established that my physical body is not separate from others, as the creation of me is dependent on the actions of my parents. The knowledge I've attained is also not mine, because as Sir Isaac Newton once said, "If I have seen further [than others] it is by standing on the shoulders of giants." I know what I know because of what others know. This is because that is.

It is impossible to completely separate the "me" from the "not me." There is very little if anything at all that I can call "me" or "mine," because of the nature of my interdependent co-arising. I am neither my biggest accomplishments nor my greatest failures.

Envisioning our interconnectedness to everything around us takes practice, as it is not our natural propensity. From the moment we wake up and throughout our daily lives, we function by thinking about "my" needs and what is happening to "me." These experiences I perceive as happening "to me" are very real—I can see, hear, and feel my experiences. Each moment seems to prove more and more that I am my own individual self, especially the big moments—getting married, delivering my children, all seem to prove that "I" am real, as in unchanging and solid.

There is nothing wrong with functioning this way; in fact, if we were not able to differentiate ourselves from others, we would really not be effective in getting anything done. There are obvious benefits in recognizing our bodies as our bodies so that we can feed it, clothe it, and take care of it properly. We obviously need to be able to recognize our children and others as having their own selves and their own needs. The point here is not that we should aim to blur the lines so that we neglect ourselves or others. Instead, we should aim to remind ourselves through mindfulness and meditation our deeply rooted connection to everyone and everything else. We should be more skillful in the way we relate to ourselves so that we include all that we are.

Emptiness is not a void; it is fullness. It is full of potential, full of opportunity, full of change and growth. Viewing the world from an emptiness perspective is liberating. The chains that we have tied ourselves down will disappear, and we discover a more authentic, flexible, compassionate way of living. We learn to be more creative in our healing, and we see open doors that we couldn't see before. We no longer see ourselves as one fixed thing; we no longer feel tied to one existence, as we can see clearly that our permanent self is just an illusion.

By realizing and cultivating emptiness, we grow seeds of compassion for all other beings. The recognition that our survival is contingent upon the well-being of others and of the earth can breed a loving awareness of their struggles and motivate a passion for kindness and empathy. We see that our suffering is not unique, that others suffer as well, and that awareness nurtures the seeds of compassion.

Through the lens of emptiness, I can see that taking care of the earth is taking care of me and is taking care of you. When I am mindful of my negative impact on the earth, I am mindful of my negative impact on you. When I am taking gentle care of the earth, I am taking gentle care of you.

Gratitude begins to grow where there is awareness of emptiness. I am grateful for the sun for its warmth, the sky for its spaciousness, the rivers for their nourishment. I am grateful for the farmer who grows my food, the truck driver who delivers it, and the construction worker who builds safe roads. I am grateful for the bees that pollinate the flowers and keep the ecosystem alive. I am grateful for the ants that turn and aerate the soil. I feel a deep gratitude for all things and everyone, as I can see how everything is connected; everything gives rise to everything else.

Humans don't naturally operate with an emptiness mindset, which causes us a lot of suffering. However, for survival reasons, it becomes clear why it is necessary for us to recognize our own individual needs. I need to recognize and be able to differentiate my body from the rest of the world so I can survive. But we tend to often take our own individual needs too far; we tend to confuse our needs with wants, our craving for more as a necessity.

We cling to our achievements, waving them around with pride as if they belong to only us. We take more than we need, because we are biologically primed to fear not having enough, even though most of us are not living in scarcity. Our behaviors are such because of our biological priming for survival and our lack of awareness of our connection to everyone and everything else in the universe.

We stifle our individual growth based on our perceived limitations, the perception we have of the boundaries of ourselves. We struggle to see ourselves in anything beyond our fingers and toes. Somewhere along the path, we have forgotten that we are the earth, that we are everything. Thich Nhat Hanh illuminated emptiness by describing a wave that, as it rises up and then begins its descent back into the ocean, recognizes that although its current form is a wave its true nature is the ocean, which it will inevitably return to. We are all waves in the same ocean.

Suffering arises when we deny or are ignorant of our true nature, our deep connection to all things. We spend so much of our lives chasing things that we believe will make us more special, more unique, more worthy of love and belonging. We chase these things because we've forgotten how perfect we already are, just being a wave.

We put ourselves in little boxes and expect ourselves to grow. We think we are keeping ourselves safe, but safe from what? We are scared of the unknown, scared to experience an existence outside of the familiar, tiny space we have come to call our "selves." We have convinced ourselves that we are a certain way, that our lives are a certain way, and we make choices based on the confined version we have decided to be. We tend to make the same mistakes, the same choices that bring the same suffering, because we've told ourselves that's all there is for us, and this is how we are.

Turning only toward pleasant experiences, we tend to deny any part of us that creates discomfort. We think that by highlighting all of our "specialness," we will be better off than others. We so deeply fear not being enough that we deny the parts of us that don't seem to fit into our idea of perfection.

When we look at nature, we see that it opens its arms to everything—to the beautiful, the ugly, the thriving, and the dying. Trees communicate their needs to other trees through the mycelium underground. When one tree suffers, the other trees come to help. Trees recognize their shared existence. When an animal dies in the forest, scavenger animals eat the flesh, and the earth takes the rest, and the decomposing body nourishes the soil and transforms into new growth, new beginnings.

Like the earth, we can open our arms to all things, our pleasure and our pain, and the pleasure and pain of others. Where pain and discomfort exist, there lies an opportunity for transformation; denying its existence doesn't make it any less real. By acknowledging all parts of us, we open so many doors of opportunity.

Acknowledging all the parts of us can be incredibly difficult, particularly if we have had traumatic experiences in our lives, whether it was the way we were raised or any specific traumatic event. We may feel unsafe acknowledging those wounded parts of ourselves, especially if they trigger strong, unpleasant emotions. It is helpful to remind ourselves that although these events have had a huge negative impact on us, they do not define us. We are not serving our individual growth, however, by ignoring them. Only by acknowledging every part of ourselves can we truly set ourselves free.

Emptiness also illuminates things as they actually are, without the stories we add to things. We are all great storytellers in our own lives, but the stories we create cause so much unnecessary suffering. We look for meaning where there is no meaning; we hunt for clues that seem to prove our stories are true. We tend to feel safer where there are answers, so we create them ourselves where there is ambiguity.

When a tree in a forest is diseased or damaged, it doesn't make up painful stories about why this unfortunate thing has happened to it. The tree doesn't tell itself things like, "Oh, this must have happened to me because I'm not a good enough tree; the other trees must hate me." As it lacks a human brain and consciousness, the tree is able to take care of its wound without complicating and worsening its suffering.

Humans, on the other hand, intensify their suffering by telling themselves futile stories about how their lives should go and why they are suffering. Instead of recognizing our wounds and healing them, we let them fester with the stories we tell. We think things like "Bad things keep happening to me. My marriage is suffering right now, I must be a bad partner. My job is overwhelming, I must not be smart or capable enough." We have unrealistic expectations of ourselves and punish ourselves when we fail to measure up. We get stuck in these stories and let them define how we ultimately experience our lives. We eventually forget that we have put ourselves in a box, and we lack creativity when it comes to healing our own suffering.

Emptiness can be a great teacher when there is suffering in our lives. We recognize that our perceived failures are not fundamentally who we are. There are so many causes and conditions that have led us to where we are in our lives at this very moment. Life is complex, and telling ourselves stories about our unworthiness gives us no space to grow.

Emptiness reminds us that we are not just one thing, not just one existence, and that our true nature is that we are everything. Being that we are everything, we don't have to confine ourselves to the little "I" anymore. We see everyone and everything as a part of us, and by healing the world, we heal ourselves. We remember that other options are available, other solutions, other ways of being. As I see my nature to be interdependent, I no longer feel alone. My suffering is the world's suffering; my thriving is the world's thriving.

Being in the climate crisis that we are currently in, we seem to have forgotten our emptiness and our interdependence. So many people are stuck in the little "I" that they forget that the world's suffering is their suffering. The polluted and overfished oceans, the destruction of rainforests and increased carbon emissions, are all confirmation that we have forgotten our true nature. We are hurting ourselves by hurting the earth. It's difficult to conceive of our connection to all the pollution, to all the destruction of the earth, when we are living our daily lives inside our little "I's." Because we are so far removed from a lot of the suffering we cause, we feel less connected and responsible for the suffering we are causing. When we take care of the earth, the earth takes care of us; we are the earth.

The good news is this: because we are the cause of much of our own suffering, we are also the best healers of our suffering. Emptiness lights the path that allows us to become unbound to the existence we have tied ourselves to. We are able to live more in the present moment, without adding painful stories and beliefs to each situation, and make more skillful decisions. The Persian poet Rumi said, "There's nothing to believe. Only when I quit believing in myself did I come into this beauty… Day and night I guarded the pearl of my soul. Now in this ocean of pearling currents, I've lost track of which was mine."

Emptiness allows us to recognize ourselves in all other beings and begin to heal ourselves and the world around us. Our partner's healing is our healing. The earth's healing is our healing. I am my parents, I am the river, I am the plants, I am the sky. The dissolution of the boundaries I created for my "self" has opened me to a world of a deeper, more connected, more authentic existence.

****

Awareness Exercise:

1. Begin a meditation practice on thoughts and limiting beliefs:

    Our minds are always active; thinking is its function. But when we don't recognize thoughts and beliefs as simply functions of the mind, we fall into the trap of believing at all, causing us to suffer. Many of our core beliefs are driven by our earliest hurts and fears. What would life be like for us if we didn't believe every thought we had?

    In the words of Islamic scholar and poet Rumi, "Why do you stay in prison when the door is so wide open? Move outside the tangle of fear thinking. The entrance door to the sanctuary is inside you."

Guided Meditation on Thoughts and Limiting Beliefs:

Begin by finding a comfortable seated position. Allow your eyes to close or rest half open in a slight downward gaze and begin to rest in the present moment. Scan the body from head to toe, releasing any obvious tension.

Consider taking in a couple of deep cleansing breaths, then allow the breath to be natural.

Without needing control over it, notice how the body breathes itself.

Notice how the breath changes. Sometimes it's short and shallow; sometimes it's long and deep.
Now bring your awareness to the pause at the end of the in-breath and out-breath. Like a cat, patiently waiting for a mouse to come out of the hole, notice when the body breathes in and out, as the body naturally will.

Ask yourself, "Who is the one that is breathing?" The body breathing itself.

After a while, you might notice that you've gotten lost in thoughts. When this happens, consider softly naming the content of your thoughts to yourself: "Judging, planning, worrying, or simply, thinking," and then return your attention to the breath.

Notice how the mind naturally thinks.

Ask yourself, "Who is the one that is thinking?" The mind thinking itself. The body breathes. The mind thinks. These are simply functions of the body and mind.

Now bring your attention to any limiting beliefs that may be present today or that you often struggle with—any judgmental beliefs about yourself such as "I'm not good enough," "I'm doing this wrong," "I'm unworthy of love." Notice what it feels like to hold this belief, what it feels like in the body.

Recognize that this belief is a product of the mind, just like a thought. There's no need to be angry at the mind. Beliefs like this are the mind's way of protecting itself. Our core beliefs are often rooted in fear—fear of being left out, fear of not getting what we need. You can consider saying to yourself, "Thank you for being here. I know you came to protect me, but I'm okay. I don't need you."

The mind creates beliefs.

Now ask yourself, "Is it *possible* that even though I hold this belief, it isn't actually *true*?"

The mind thinks, but we don't have to follow the thoughts. The mind creates beliefs, but we don't have to hold them.

Ask yourself, "Who would I be if I didn't hold this belief?"

Consider placing a hand on your heart and tell yourself, "I am safe. I am enough. I am worthy of love and belonging."

For the last couple of minutes, gently return the attention to the breath. Notice anything that arises as simply products of the body and mind.

Journal Exercise:

1. What did it feel like to bring doubt to your limiting beliefs?
2. Who would you be if you didn't hold your limiting beliefs?

Chapter 9: Aimlessness

Radical acceptance rests on letting go of the illusion of control and a willingness to notice and accept things as they are right now, without judging.

—Tara Brach

Tiny flickers of light dance through the dark forest. The chatter of friendly voices flows through the huddles of warm bodies on a cold, fall evening. Many of the faces appear familiar in this glowing stream of gatherers.

The teacher passes to each child the lantern they had made in school. Everly smiles and holds up her little glass lantern, decorated with colored paper and fit with a starry handle, holding a tealight candle inside.

"Wow, Everly," I say to her, "It's absolutely beautiful."

Jack totes his tall paper lantern from a couple of years ago when he was in preschool. Jack and Everly find a couple of their friends, and the four of them dance around in a circle, an array of giggles and sparkles.

The story of Martinmas goes that a man named St. Martin discovered a homeless man shivering on a cold, dark night, and he offered him a piece of his cloak for warmth. Later that evening, St. Martin was visited by an angel in his dream. Donning his cloak, the angel illuminated to him his calling to serve those who are less fortunate. St. Martin devoted the rest of his life to serving others, becoming a patron saint to poor people and outcasts of society. He was revered for his kindness and his ability to bring warmth and light to those in need.

One evening during the darkest month of the year, some people gather with glowing lanterns and walk together, symbolizing our inner light that we must carry into the darkness. Like St. Martin, we too carry a warmth and light that we can share with those in need. In the cold, in the darkness, where nature sleeps, we must be wakeful.

"Shhh," I hush the kids. "It's starting."

Displaying poise and reverence of people much older than them, the children stop giggling and bring their attention to the teacher leading the ceremony. A tiny hand slips into mine, and we take slow steps behind her, following her lead in journey and song.

I go with my little lantern,
My lantern goes with me.

With each step, I reflect on all the causes and conditions it took for this moment to be. My childhood—all the good and all the bad. Moving away from home. Going to nursing school, meeting Alex. Getting my degree, getting married. Having children.

In heaven the stars are shining,
On Earth are shining we.

I recall how in many of those stages of my life I have been living in the future. I have not spent much time just being where I am. How's a goal-oriented person to do that anyhow? "I'll be happy when…" has been a common theme of my life. But with each goal reached, a new peak revealed itself. It's all been an illusion.

My light shines bright,
in darkest night,

Life is only in the present moment. This moment, this *exact* moment, will never *be* again. Constantly running after success, for happiness somewhere else at some other time, is a grave mistake in missing out on the experience of life. How I live right now is how I live my life.

La bimba, la bumba, la boom
Boom, boom!

Yet it still pulls me, an ever-present force, to constantly be thinking about where I'm *going* instead of being where I *am*. This is what my culture has bred into me. How to reconcile? How to have goals, to have aspirations, but to hold them lightly?

My light shines bright,
in darkest night,

We've been trained to believe that striving equates to living. Be well educated! Get your degree! Make a lot of money! Be in your best physical shape! Get married! Have a positive attitude! Have children! Be the best mother or father! Keep pushing! Keep pushing! Keep pushing! And we've been trained to answer the most impossible question of all: "Who are you?"

> *La bimba, la bumba, la boom*
> *Boom, boom!*

We gather at the foot of the willow tree while the teacher sings a story. I hear, but I don't listen. My attention is on the beautiful, shining faces of all the people here. Although I don't know them all, I am connected to them all. My existence is interconnected, my path intertwined. I secretly whisper to myself my wish for all of these people and for all people, to recognize how beautiful they are, just as they are. That they don't need to go anywhere or "become" anything to be worthy of love and belonging.

****

Aimlessness is the third door of liberation. It illustrates a way of living that recognizes that the greatest goal is being present right here, right now. It suggests that by focusing too strongly on our goals, we will inevitably miss out on the true wonder and glory of our lives. Aimlessness is not to live without aspirations but rather to hold those goals lightly and to enjoy the process of life unfolding itself.

There is an old story about a fisherman who, after a successful morning, is relaxing on the beach next to his fishing pole. An American tourist comes up to him and asks, "What are you doing? Why aren't you fishing?"

The fisherman replies, "I fished all morning and was very successful. I sold all my fish to the market, and now I am relaxing on the beach."

The American responds, "Well then, why don't you get out there and fish some more?"

The fisherman says, "What will my reward be?"

"More money, of course, to buy bigger nets and catch more fish," the American says, appearing confused.

"And then what will my reward be?" asks the fisherman.
"You'll be able to buy a boat and catch even more fish, and make even more money," the American answers matter-of-factly.

"And then what will my reward be?" the fisherman asks again.

"You can buy a bigger boat and hire people to work for you," answers the American, getting frustrated.

"And then what will my reward be?" the fisherman repeats.

"Don't you understand?! You'll be able to buy a whole fleet of ships and hire people to do all the fishing for you. Then you can spend the rest of your days sitting on the beach, without a care in the world!" the American proclaims, clearly exasperated.

The fisherman simply smiles and responds, "Well, that is what I am doing now." He lies back down and rests in the sun, eyes closed.

In a culture where we are bred to constantly *strive* for things—for fame, for fortune, and for expertise, the concept of aimlessness might seem uninspiring and irresponsible. But some important questions we must ask ourselves are: What are we striving for? What do we believe this will bring us? And last, what conditions of happiness are available to us right here, right now?

We've been conditioned to believe that happiness is something that can only be obtained through titles, educational degrees, social positioning, and economic status. We're disillusioned with the belief that happiness is reserved for some time in the future: when we've paid off our debts, when our children are sleeping through the night, when we lose those ten pounds, when we're on vacation, when we retire. But what conditions of happiness are available to us right now? And how does how we think of ourselves play a role in that?

Perhaps ever since we were young children, people have been asking us, "What are you going to *be* when you grow up?" It's been driven into our minds that we need to "become" someone. It creates an undercurrent of the "not enough as I am" thought in our minds. So we start striving. We strive for labels to decorate ourselves with, not realizing that we already have what we're searching for.

Our inherent worthiness can neither be obtained nor lost; we were born with it. Even before our first breath, "we" existed. We are our ancestors, we are the earth, and we hold intrinsic value. Thich Nhat Hanh teaches, "Nowhere to go, nothing to do." There is nothing we need or do and no one we need to "become" to be worthy of love and belonging. That is available to us right here, right now.

Self-improvement is still possible, and actually more achievable, when we recognize our intrinsic worthiness. Shunryu Suzuki says, "Each of you is perfect the way you are… and you can use a little improvement." This paradoxical statement acknowledges our inherent value, while also recognizing that we can all do work to improve ourselves. But the work we need to do and the mistakes we make do not negate our worthiness.

The three doors of liberation, signlessness, emptiness, and aimlessness, help us transcend dualistic notions. Birth and death, sameness and otherness, good and bad are the bedrock of all suffering. Nirvana is not some place to get to; it is available to each of us right here and now. Nirvana is the space we dwell in once we realize and pass through these three doors.

****

"What is your purpose?" Daniel Greening, a friend and fellow secular Buddhist practitioner, asks me during our writing club one day.

"To become an author and a mindfulness teacher," I reply quickly and confidently.

"Those are goals," Dan kindly explains. "What is your purpose?"

I pause for a moment. I've always been a very goal-oriented person. Make it there, obtain that degree, finish that project. It's motivating, yes, but it always pulls me out of where I am. It feeds into the illusion that happiness and success are in the future, anywhere else but here.

I ask myself, "Why am I doing this, and why do I care?" I reflect for a moment on what is driving me down this path.

"To help people… To make mindfulness practices more accessible." The answer flows through me.

I can live my purpose every day, in each moment. I don't have to wait for some time in the future to live it. Each moment I respond compassionately to my children when they are exploding, pause instead of reacting to my partner, and show compassion to myself when I fail to do all these things, I am living my purpose. Focusing first on my purpose keeps me right here, right now, living in a way that aligns with my values.

I still have goals—finish this book, finish my mindfulness program and begin teaching mindfulness, and grow my YouTube channel. But my relationship with my goals is loose and flexible. If I don't reach my goals, but I'm still living my purpose, I'm succeeding.

Like the lens of a camera, I can zoom in and zoom out on my life and the choices I make. I can zoom in and really be present with whoever I'm with and whatever I'm doing. I try to spend most of my time zoomed in. Then I can zoom out to gain a wider view of my life and determine whether or not I'm still headed in the direction I wish to go. Then when I get sucked back into the trance of life, impulsively plowing forward, I hop off my hamster wheel and ask myself, "Where am I? What did it take for this moment to be?"

Like so many others, I grew up believing that I needed to do something or be something to be worthy of love and belonging. I've often felt as if the main purpose of my bastardized existence was to make them feel worthy of love and belonging. And in that pillage, I lost the ability to see my own worthiness. If you search outside to fix what's broken inside, these walls might cave in on you if you go perusing.

I used to be angry at them. I used to blame them for doing this to me. But that anger was a burden that eventually became too heavy to bear. I set it down and looked inside it. I saw that, like me, they too suffer. Like me, they too have been hurt. Like me, they too want to feel loved and accepted. I'm not angry anymore. My heart broke open a long time ago, and sadness and hurt came rushing out. It took years to process, and now what's left is compassion.

I see behind their veil of anger is a desperate longing for love and understanding. I see their goodness; it's always been there, as has mine, buried under unskillful action fueled by confusion. We are beautiful and worthy of love and belonging, even with all of our scars. Our worthiness is tied to no conditions.

At the core of all our striving is a longing to feel accepted, understood, and loved. The only thing we need to do is realize that we are already worthy of love and belonging. There are no titles we need to gain in order to obtain it; it is already ours.

The label of "bad mom" plagued me for years. It was paralyzing. I mistakenly believed that by trying to be "perfect" I could achieve a "good mom" status. But experience taught me that it was an uphill race with no finish line.

We can exercise more skillful relationships with our labels by loosening our attachment to them. I now tell people that "I work as a nurse," "I practice secular Buddhism," and I will soon say "I teach mindfulness." This allows me to comprehend the full manifestation of my being, allowing for changes in the roles in my lifetime. I feel less attached to the labels and less identified with them. Practicing emptiness for me means dwelling in the spaciousness of having no concrete identifiable "self." In this space, there are more possibilities, more opportunity for growth, and less space for the stasis that shame causes. I can hold myself responsible for the mistakes I make and work on doing better, because I no longer see a single, separate "me" to shame.

I look into the mirror and I see myself. I see hazel eyes, light brown hair, fair skin, smile lines, and crow's feet just beginning to make their appearance. I look so *real*, and of course, I am—in the physical, practical sense. But I am also empty—empty of a separate self. When I look into the mirror a second time, I also see you, my ancestors, my children, my partner, the food that I eat, the air that I breathe, the river that flows through the city I live in. I see the whole world.

I still get lost in the race of life. I still get caught up in striving and self-judgment. I still find myself chasing labels. I want to get this book published and "become" an author. I want to finish my mindfulness program and "become" a teacher. But now, I find that I can more frequently wake up from the trance of separateness.

I know that once I get this book published, and once I gain the title of mindfulness teacher, a new peak will reveal itself to me. There is no end to this game. So as much as I can, I live my purpose, right here and now.

After all, when the striving arises, I have to ask myself, "Where am I going?" And what's more, "*Who* is going?"

References

Brown, Brené. *Daring Greatly: How the Courage to Be Vulnerable Transforms the Way We Live, Love, Parent, and Lead*. Sheridan, WY: Gotham Books, 2012, p. 69.

Budiarto, Yohanes, and Avin Fadilla Helmi. "Shame and Self-esteem: A Meta-Analysis." *Europe's Journal of Psychology*, vol. 17, no. 2, Leibniz Institute for Psychology (ZPID), May 2021, pp. 131–45, https://doi.org/10.5964/ejop.2115.

DeFelipe, Javier. "The Evolution of the Brain, the Human Nature of Cortical Circuits, and Intellectual Creativity." *Frontiers in Neuroanatomy*, vol. 5, 16 May 2011, pp. 1–2, https://doi.org/10.3389/fnana.2011.00029.

Fox, Kieran C.R., et al. "Is Meditation Associated with Altered Brain Structure? A Systematic Review and Meta-Analysis of Morphometric Neuroimaging in Meditation Practitioners." *Neuroscience & Biobehavioral Reviews*, vol. 43, June 2014, pp. 48–73, https://doi.org/10.1016/j.neubiorev.2014.03.016.

Kim, Dongbeom, et al. "Mechanisms Contributing to the Induction and Storage of Pavlovian Fear Memories in the Lateral Amygdala." *Learning & Memory*, vol. 20, no. 8, July 2013, pp. 421–30, https://doi.org/10.1101/lm.030262.113.

Neff, Kristin D. "Self-Compassion: Theory, Method, Research, and Intervention." *Annual Review of Psychology*, vol. 74, no. 1, 2023, pp. 193–218, https://doi.org/10.1146/annurev-psych-032420-031047.

Newberg, Andrew B., et al. "Cerebral Blood Flow Differences between Long-Term Meditators and Non-Meditators." *Consciousness and Cognition*, vol. 19, no. 4, Dec. 2010, pp. 899–905, https://doi.org/10.1016/j.concog.2010.05.003.

Northoff, Georg, et al. "Self-Referential Processing in Our Brain—A Meta-Analysis of Imaging Studies on the Self." *NeuroImage*, vol. 31, no. 1, 2006, pp. 440–57, *Crossref*, https://doi.org/10.1016/j.neuroimage.2005.12.002.

Rilling, J., "Comparative Primate Neurobiology and the Evolution of Brain Language Systems." *Current Opinion in Neurobiology*, vol. 28, 2014, pp. 1–3.

Veer, Ilya M., et al. "Beyond Acute Social Stress: Increased Functional Connectivity between Amygdala and Cortical Midline Structures." *NeuroImage*, vol. 57, no. 4, 15 Aug. 2011, pp. 1534–41, https://doi.org/10.1016/j.neuroimage.2011.05.074.

About the Author

Heather Schenck works as a mindfulness meditation teacher and registered nurse. She is passionate about teaching mindfulness and other secular Buddhist concepts, and making these teachings more accessible. She has had a dedicated mindfulness practice with the support of a secular Buddhist sangha since 2020. She lives in Colorado with her partner and two kids.